The best team wins
JHON ALBART

Table of Contents

The best team wins 1
JHON ALBART 1
Lesson n. 1. NDA 7
Lesson n. 2. Timing 11
Lesson n. 3. Execution 24
Lesson n. 4. Business model 58
Lesson n. 5. Liquid business 102
Lesson n. 6 Business accelerator 127
Lesson n. 7. Fundraising 162
Lesson n. 8. Overselling 193
Lesson n. 9. Elevator pitch 206
Lesson n. 10. Sales pitch 222
Lesson n. 11. Networking 275
Lesson n. 12. Exit 288

The book

This book is the bible of those who want to create a startup in Italy. It answers all the questions of those who have an idea and want to turn it into a millionaire business and, above all, reveals the tricks of the trade to achieve success. But there is more. It lists all the mistakes not to make, offers the "map" to follow and gives detailed instructions that every aspiring startupper must know. Can you draw up an NDA? Do you know when to propose it? Could you sustain a

"Elevator pitch"? Do you know the difference between first, second and third rounds and the rules of conduct when meeting a venture capitalist? Are you able to write a business plan or present your business model in a convincing way? And the formula for achieving a financeable execution? Do you know where to find the first 100,000 euros and who to ask for further funding? Well: Startup in 21 days will not just give you all the tips, but will make you live. It is a complete and detailed manual, written as a story that will accompany readers in the creation of their company: we will peek into the

"rooms of power", we will take part in meetings where
«Things happen», we will witness the drafting of the plan and we will have access to the same worksheets as those who are already building their project. An essential reading for anyone who wants to create a startup or even just understand how this world works!

Lesson n. 1. NDA

Never start from that!
March 1st - 11.30 am, venture capitalist's office

We went in and sat down. The man who would decide our fate was standing in front of us. At the desk sat a younger boy in a suit and tie that we had never seen: his son, a partner, his lawyer, a manager... What would it have changed for us to know? Nothing: after all we were nothingness; nullity with an idea worth millions of euros, however.
The young man broke the silence. "Well, tell us a little who you are and why we should finance you."
"We have an idea that will forever revolutionize the way we interact with social networks."
"Sounds good to me," said the man with the money. "What is it about?"
"Well, before we expose it to you, we'd like to submit a little gentlemen's agreement." We were prepared: my partner's uncle had prepared an NDA; 1 might not have impressed them, but it

would make it clear they weren't dealing with
of the unwary.
The old man snorted, picked up the paper, didn't even look at it and passed it to the young man who evaluated it hastily. "Take care of it," he said.
"Good," the boy began. "Things don't work like that: you can't propose to a venture capitalist to sign a non-compete agreement in the dark. We understand your reasons, but what if we were already financing an idea similar to yours or if one of our projects was by chance rethought and transformed into an application that does the things you think of? This, "he concluded, returning the NDA to us," just makes you look naive. "
I was stunned, annoyed and annoyed: I had insisted on preparing that document and I had every reason. Did we serve him an idea worth millions of euros on a tray and didn't we have to protect ourselves from the risk of having it stolen? And, moreover, to be defined as naïve because we were afraid of being deceived? What would happen to us if you stole the idea instead ?! I thought; but I remained silent, just looking at him with distrust. The young man stared at me insistently and I

didn't understand why.

"I understand your fears, but in this way you give the impression that, besides the idea, you have nothing else. Now tell us what else you have. "
Those words clarified the point: we had nothing. We didn't make the mistake of looking at each other before sketching out an impromptu answer. And this anyway
"Friend of the venture" had not uttered even three sentences that I already felt a sincere hatred for him.
"We have developed the project." They looked at me suspiciously. "We're at 80% ..." I hastened to specify, "but it's not too long for a working beta."

"That's a good thing," the young man said. The man with the money snorted again, like someone who'd gotten the wrong dish at a restaurant after a long wait. The boy turned to him: "If you allow, I would like to continue with them, in my office."
"You waste your time," the older man replied as if we weren't even there. There was already a wall between us and him, and soon there would be another.

Lesson n. 1

Setting the deal by asking for a confidentiality agreement will only make you appear naive.

1 NDA stands for Non-disclosure agreement: it is a confidentiality agreement.

Lesson n. 2. Timing

Your only asset
March 1st - 11.35 am, moved to a smaller office

"Let me make one point clear before moving on. 99% of match 1s that begin by submitting a confidentiality agreement end with that sentence. "
"Are we the 1%?" I dared to ask.
"No. The 1% are those who actually have the conditions to propose such a pre-agreement. But they are few. " He looked at us. "And not you, anyway," he added to make us understand to what extent we were nothingness.
"But then why didn't you send us away right away?" As I finished the sentence, I realized the gaffe; he dropped it. Instead, he answered the question we should have asked.
"If you had invented a machine capable of regressing a pancreatic tumor, or the chemical formula for regrowing hair, then you would have something that can be protected by law, but when it comes to ideas and how to apply them , the law cannot protect our thoughts: there are endless ways in which we could change

your idea and make it seem ours. This is why in your case there is no point in proposing an NDA, and this is why you made an amateur mistake. "

I was silent for the second time; but now it was a heavy and conscious silence. Maybe we were dealing with a master of words, but our lightness, summarized in those few, simple sentences, appeared embarrassingly evident.

«So, the situation is the following: you need money to realize your revolutionary idea, but you cannot tell it around otherwise you risk that it will be stolen from you; and even supposing to find someone as foolish as you, willing to sign a blank confidentiality agreement without knowing what it is ... I am sure that any lawyer will be able to confirm that the legal value of such an agreement is almost nil: too easy to circumvent , and very few holds to prove in court that the idea was yours from the start. At this point, I know you are wondering, so I ask you: how do you protect yourself from the risk of someone stealing your idea while you tell it around to finance it? "

We didn't know.

"The only way you can protect yourself from the theft of your idea ..." followed an overly studied pause, "is to move faster than anyone who will find out!"

Captain Obvious 2's voice rang in my head: Is that all ?! Just this? Hurry to realize the idea before someone else does? It seemed so. And it didn't seem like a genius tip at all. I liked this guy less and less.

"Once the idea is financed, you will be protected, but only by those who financed you."

The urge to insult him was abruptly blocked by that clarification. "Wait up:

Does this mean that, at any moment, even after having built it, a multinational could decide to copy the idea from scratch, without anything being done to prevent it ?! "

"No, it's not exactly like that ... but it comes very close, in fact," he said. Then he paused for thought as if he were mentally evaluating the words to use to better discourage us. «They can realize a very similar idea, change something... maybe improve the defects... and then make you a ruthless and bloody competition. And even if you take them to court and win a case, well... you know

Has Samsung stopped producing smartphones ?! " 3

"Crazy stuff!" I exclaimed.

My snooty mentor smiled in amusement with the expression of someone about to play the joke: "Welcome to my world."

"Let's put it this way: what prevents you and me or any millionaire company, including this one, from copying the idea of Google, YouTube or Facebook, creating a better version of it and competing with them?"

"I would say lack of money and time: the companies you mentioned have existed for longer and have millions of users: they start with a huge competitive advantage, plus they have mountains of dollars on their side."

My know-it-all mentor nodded satisfied: the obvious answer to that rhetorical question of his was in agreement. «An almost virtually unbridgeable advantage, because they grow exponentially, that's right! The fact that they started earlier and the speed with which they have

being able to move, expand and then monetize 4 made the difference! " A pause followed.

"Well. This is your asset. " 5

Now I was confused.

«Wait: our asset? You mean theirs... because it doesn't seem to me that money and time are exactly our strength. "
"It has to become like this: you have no choice!"
He jumped forward and began to smile reassuringly, and I doubted that he was a dangerous person and that we weren't exactly in his room to get help.
«The only asset you can count on is to leave before the others and to move faster. Believe me: if your idea is worth anything at all, there are at least two thousand other brains in India and China who are already thinking about it, testing and improving it, correcting any errors. And I didn't say two hundred, but two thousand: I never joke about the numbers. The only advantage you have in getting ahead of them is timing, i.e. the speed at which you will be able to penetrate the market. And it just depends on how fast you decide to move from now on. At present, your advantage is getting smaller and smaller, each time you stop to think about how ingenious and revolutionary your idea is, wasting time protecting yourself from those who could steal it from you. So my advice is: act now!

I was beginning to get nervous: he hadn't asked us for anything yet, but it was as if my girlfriend's gynecologist was asking me if I was ready to be a father.

I braked sharply to shake him off. "So we should risk letting you cheat the idea, for fear that two thousand Indochinese who don't even know us will do it?"
"Exact."
He said it like this, without flinching; he was very serious and detached, as if my ironic joke was a serious and pertinent reflection, rather than sarcastic. The result was that I became serious too.
"Seriously, let me understand: do you think the best strategy for a startupper is to cross your fingers and hope they don't steal your idea while trying to make it happen?"
"No, the best strategy is to move your ass before someone takes your seat." He remained serious and calm, but he stared at my chair.
"But..."
"If your idea is good, someone will realize it sooner or later: give yourself the chance to be you, is it so difficult to understand?"
"But ..." I said again.

He pointed to the clock on the wall. "Tic-tac-tic-tac ... All around you you can observe the time, the only real asset for each of us, which tapers more and more until the moment when we all die."

That sentence was out of register, but it was unexpectedly effective in getting me to focus on what was really important. «Ok, ok... if it comes to competing with someone who has no money like me, I understand your advice; But tell me this: against a company like yours, how could I even think I am faster? Out of the teeth, my question is: how can we be trusted? Once we tell you how our idea works, it will be as if you were traveling in a helicopter while we travel in a small car; it wouldn't be an equal competition! "

In response, he smiled.

"It's your fault that he's not on equal terms."

"My fault?"

"Do you understand why?"

"No," I replied sincerely.

"You sat at the right table, but you did it too soon. You met the backers and had your first match when you weren't ready yet. You cannot sit at this table, the negotiating table, armed only with a good idea. There is a reason why the highest stakes banks all have a minimum bet at the casino: the big players leave no room for maneuver for newbies. When you have only the idea, no matter how good, you have nothing to deal with. And since an idea is no longer worth anything after you share it, you risk burning it. You know this and your lenders know it. The only thing you can hope for is that a company like ours has so many things to think about that it is considered unprofitable to steal the idea from those who are willing to devote time and resources to develop it,

"Should we offer you a joint venture ?!"

He smiled again. «Here is another misconception that proves to me once more that you are amateurs. You are not structured enough to propose a joint venture: you should already be on the market, with your company behind you, producing

useful. To be clear: when I say 'our project', I really mean a project of our property; a business controlled by us, which also involves you, to a small extent. "

I wanted to leave and slam the door but, for some reason I didn't understand, I checked myself. "So you advise me to come back when I'm ready?" To try again when I have something more concrete in hand? To take the smallest steps first? "

"Yes, it would be wise," he commented, looking at me with an air of pity. "Too bad you have no idea what the steps to take before meeting a venture capitalist are. You know nothing, you are a clean slate. You're a cabal joke who happened to win the worst lottery of his life. I mean... going looking for a venture capitalist too soon was a mistake, sure, but your real curse is that you managed to find one! It is not at all frequent: if I may be suspicious ... what is your secret? Are you the son of a friend of a friend? However it doesn't matter! You walked into this office twenty minutes ago, and how long did it take you to burn yourself completely ?! Personally, I already dumped you at hello. "

I opened my mouth to point out something, but nothing came out.

"The only reason I'm still talking to you, the reason we moved into my office, is that you are still 'moldable', and that excites me."

I nodded at regular intervals. He had said "moldable" ... perhaps he meant to make me his anti-stress pose ?!

"Whatever you propose to do, at this point, you will never have the strength to refuse it. You smelled the smell of the rooms where things happen: here startups become successful case histories, and you are dying to stay there, to become one of those stories. To answer your question: of course you should go back and decide to do things sequentially, take all the steps in the right order, and it would be by far the most sensible thing to do ... but the problem is that you don't have the no idea what those steps are."

Was it true or was he just having fun with me? Were there any steps to take first? Had I fallen victim to corporate sadism? Would he have made a rug out of me by pretending to forge me as his protégé ?! I was understanding little, but I was fascinated by the picture that appeared. Light years from the impression I thought I had given, eons of what I had planned, "in a galaxy far, far away," my conviction that I was looking like a shrewd negotiator vanished swallowed up by black holes. Meanwhile, he too was on his trip: a lucid and mathematical trip.

"Let's face it: even if you could choose - and you can't - you would never want to go back, because the prospect of receiving a loan from us is too tempting for you, so now you should look me in the eye and convince yourself that I am worthy of the your trust; after that you can only hope that I find your idea interesting enough to invest something in it, but not so easy to realize that I want to do it on my own. "

Was this really the strategy of the successful startuppers? Trusting a company in a closed box, hoping it had more important things to do? No: that was the suicide strategy he was suggesting to me; he had been all too clear about this.

What was I supposed to do? I would have put away all my dreams of glory and my future hopes,

wishing her schedule was too busy to find a quarter of an hour space between ten and two to rip me off? To hear from a guy I met twenty minutes ago, yes. I tried an entrenchment on the short-term perspective.

"Let's say you decide to fully finance our startup: how do I keep control of the project?"

He saw my bluff from afar and cut it short. "It is premature to deal with this. So, would you like to tell me about your revolutionary idea? Signing the

agreement you brought us is obviously out of the question. "
Did we have a choice?
Of course: get out of the room and look for other contacts. But what would become of the timing?!
That tick-tock had begun to ring in my head.

Lesson n. 2

Talking to lenders too early is a mistake.
You can't sit at the negotiating table armed only with a good idea. When you only have the idea, your only asset is timing.
TIC Tac...
1   Match is the name of the meeting with the lenders. Usually the match is divided into three rounds, that is to say three different matches; the first lasts about ten minutes and is used to describe the business plan, the second explores it, the third is the final one and only in this we speak more specifically of numbers and agreements. During the various rounds, what is called a pitch is held, that is a sales speech (a pitcher is a fair barker and pitch is precisely his speech to the public, that "Venghino, gentlemen,

venghino" that the pitcher always repeats the same); for each round the startupper prepares a pitch of the specific duration, as we will see later.

2   Captain Obvious is a slightly bizarre superhero, the cartoon equivalent of Monsieur de Lapalisse.

3   Samsung was sued by Apple for producing iPhone-like cell phones; in 2012 Samsung lost the case and was forced to pay a billion dollars to the Cupertino house. Also in 2012 the Samsung Galaxy S III mobile phone exceeded the sales of the iPhone 4S mobile phone.

4   Monetizing means making money; the moment in which it monetizes is the moment in which the startup begins to collect.

5   An asset is a resource you can rely on: money is an asset, knowledge, skills, relationships, etc. are an asset.

Lesson n. 3. Execution

The only thing that matters
March 1st - 12.50 pm, bar outside the office

"Well, your idea is interesting. Now I tell you what problems you have. Number one, the fact that I find your idea interesting doesn't have the slightest value. It has potential, that's all; but find me only one idea that I don't have. "
"An awl to make holes in the water?" I smiled and he looked annoyed.
"One of the ten most profitable applications ever simulates the noise of a fart on the mobile phone: it has earned over 60 million dollars: do you really think that the student spirit has no market?"
I remained serious and learned not to make jokes when it came to capitalizing on an idea.
"I'll tell you more, the intuitions that were most successful didn't even have all this great potential; think of the iPad: a computer that does not have USB access and with limited memory. It does practically everything a phone already did, but with two huge flaws: it is more

bulky and does not call! Yet it was a worldwide success: could you explain to me why? "

"Why is it a tablet?"

"Tablets have been around for at least a decade and no one ever wanted them. What made the iPad a success is what you don't have ... "

«Millions of dollars for the advertising campaign? The Apple brand? "

«No and fire. No to the former because it is not enough to spend millions to make an idea work, otherwise tablets would have worked well before Jobs; fire because the Apple brand ... or rather the Steve Jobs brand ... is a consequence of what I'm talking about. "

"Self-confidence? Vision? Leadership? "

"Close up your Tony Robbins and Ken Blanchard manuals before I kick you out, and listen to me: tattoo this word in block letters in front of your eyes."

He took the napkin and wrote:

EXECUTION

"The idea behind your startup matters, but not as much as what you show you can set it in motion."

Which, incidentally, was nothing, and he would not be long in pointing it out.

"Everyone knew the iPad was going to be a hit, because behind it was the Apple team led by Steve 'I launched the Mac, the iPod and the iPhone' Jobs. That the product worked and how it was a detail, believe me; that it would be imperfect if everyone expected it, but they also knew that it would make no difference: the technicians received it coldly but the sales went through the roof and that is why

that investors follow the execution, not the value of an idea or a product. Instead what about you? What have you actually achieved so far? "

"Nothing concrete." It was useless to go around it. He took out a pen and started talking again.

"Let's make the roll call."

"The appeal?"

"Yes, do you remember the names of your classmates?"

"Classmates? ..." we were perplexed.

«My God, you must have gone to school, right ?! You will have heard the call hundreds of times, you will remember some names: tell me some. "

We stood in silence looking at him perplexed. He too remained silent looking at us.

It was a contest of nerves. The first one who speaks loses, I thought; silence followed.

"..."
"..."
"..."

"So there was ..." We wrote the names of our old companions one by one: I was amazed to remember almost all of them: I hadn't thought of some of them for a lifetime.

"Well, contact search: you know what all these guys are doing now? You will have Facebook, right? He was born for this!"

Within twenty minutes we knew everything about everyone, except why we needed that information. When the list was complete, our mentor picked it up.

"Well, now tell me who was good, who was bad and who was average."

We completed the task by putting an abbreviation next to each name: M + above average, M average, M- below average.

"Now tell me what you notice."

It was the list of our old high school classmates. There were the names, their grades and the careers they had made.

"What stands out," I said, "is that those with the highest grades don't always have the best positions... indeed, almost never, I'd say all places in the average. Instead it amazes me that some of the worst students have become successful entrepreneurs and managers."

"It shouldn't surprise you at all: more and more graduates are being hired by high school graduates. Here's an interesting stat: do you know there's a study called 'Why 10 and honors students work for smart people who didn't apply'?!"

"Wow... a big blow to our school system!"

«I disagree with those who say that the school system has several flaws: on the contrary, it works very well. Students with excellent grades work for students with poor grades, but it's in the order of things if you think about it. Having high grades doesn't mean you are better or smarter. The purpose of the school system is to educate, that is, to create controllable citizens who do not disturb too much. And, in the case of work, it serves to create employees. He who learns the lesson too well becomes an obedient slave; it works perfectly, for this reason the entrepreneurial culture is an exception: the way of thinking of the entrepreneurs is different from that of the mass and this means that they will laugh at you and take you for crazy;

had this predisposition, you would have left my office after the first ten minutes. What I want to show you is something else. "
"Thing?"
He indicated the school average of each promising pupil and his current occupation.
"This is the reason why venture capitalists don't invest in the potential of something: the potential, statistically, falls short of expectations! What is invested in are demonstrations of ability. "
"That's what you call execution, right?"
«We are Italians, and so is Massimo Marchiori. Do you know who he is? The man Google works thanks to. Do you know what makes Google work? What makes the search engine amazing that it is? PageRank ... "
"The algorithm invented by Larry Page!" I knew that.

"Are you sure Larry Page really made it up? Some argue that Marchiori, with its Hyper Search, has created the basis of the PageRank algorithm. In Silicon Valley many support him, but in Italy only nerds know him ... are you starting to understand? "

"Did they ... steal the idea ?!" It was ridiculous to even think so, let alone say it out loud.

"No, they used it to make Google. Larry Page himself loves to repeat: it's not the idea you have that matters, but how you make it happen! Good old Larry himself talks about execution. "

"I don't understand: are you saying that this guy invented the Google algorithm?"

"I don't know this, but for a long time the world of venture capitalists thought so; How much would an algorithm that works better than the one Google uses today be worth to an investor? Imagine that Massimo Marchiori came to you claiming that he wanted to create a search engine to compete with Google, thanks to the fact that he was the one who invented the algorithm at the base of Google, and that he had perfected that fantastic formula and had around us built an incredible search engine, able to work better than Google: would you invest in this project? "

"Certainly yes, it has all the premises of a successful case!"

«Exactly: premises! You invest in the premises: it is your mentality, you are a startupper! Venture capitalists, on the other hand, want a historian! This better search engine than Google already exists, it's called Volunia, a startup that never took off. Marchiori left the project in 2012 and was the disappointment of several of his fans. "

"Sin..."

"And we are talking about a genius with proven talent, a true nerd legend, who has made a very important contribution to the greatest startup of all time! Do you understand why your brilliant idea, despite the excellent premises, is not something you can invest in at present? "

"Of course: money is not invested on the good premises, but on the practical results that it has been shown to be able to bring ... this is meant by execution?"

"Precisely: and how much money is your execution worth so far? What have you done? Apart from the round of relationships that brought you here, what are you doing as entrepreneurs? Not as a startupper that means nothing: as entrepreneurs! "

The answer was: nothing. We had nothing, not even the company.

"Let me guess: the answer is very little, huh?" You haven't done anything, maybe you have hardly established a company ..."

More or less it was like that. Separate company.

"Do you think you are the only ones who believe in themselves? Do you think you are special and talented? Do you think you have charisma? Good for you, but thinking it doesn't make you special. On the contrary, it makes you trivial. By showing intelligence and self-confidence you don't suddenly become interesting for the world of venture capitalists. Nor is it the minimum standard required to enter that door because, unfortunately for you, the records are full of 'phenomena' that have burned the millions of a lender. Getting up at six in the morning will only make you a little bit interesting. Working on weekends may make you appear a little more serious than the competition, but what really makes the difference is not having an original plan, but making it work in the right time! "

"Get the right idea and make it happen, okay."

"No, no! The right idea is not part of the equation! You're too focused on the idea - the iPad was probably the wrong idea! It's not the idea: getting the idea is the easy part! Do you know what you startuppers have to put in your head? To stop idolizing the idea and start putting execution at the center! "

"But if I can't get financed when I have the right idea ... how can I do it with the wrong idea?"

«Start by realizing a trivial idea! Try to build a business from an already tested model that works. Prepare the business plan for a chain of coffee shops: do you think you can do it? "

"Cafeterias?"

"Think about it: the idea is there, it works and you already have tested models to copy ... find me only one lender who wouldn't listen to you!"

"But the cafes already exist ..."

"And with this?! It's an advantage: you can copy and take inspiration, analyze case histories, avoid mistakes. "

"Well ... it is more difficult to enter an already manned market than to create a new one!"

"Not at all! You seem convinced that making something that nobody has ever done is easier, because there is less competition, but it's not like that! "

"Right, if it has already been done, anyone can do it again ..."

"That's not true either! Succeeding in an old market has its difficulties... creating a new market has others... but you can do both as long as you apply the formula! "

"The formula? Which formula? "

"The execution formula: the one that makes you financeable in the eyes of an investor."

"No one has ever told me that there is a mathematical formula."

"I never said it's math, but it exists and I'll try to explain it to you like this: do you think doing a hundred push-ups a day makes your muscles grow?"

"Well ... yes..."

"The question is, how long does it take to complete the series?"

"I'm not following you."

"I'll go slower: forty English lessons, if you do them in forty days, they can do improve your English, but done in forty weeks, forty months or forty years, they become useless! And we are talking about the exact same lessons! The formula is..." He took his pen and wrote:

Execution = results / time.

«It is not enough to be able to bring results, you also have to bring them in interesting times. How many results are you able to bring and in how long? This is what any lenders will invest in! You are worth nothing because you have not brought reasonable results, achieved in an interesting time, to put on the plate! " This time it was I who wrote:

Reasonable results, in an interesting time.

He had made it very simple. We had the idea and we thought it was enough. It wasn't like that and now we understood it. We didn't have to accomplish everything, but before we sat down at the lenders table we should have already achieved some results, in an interesting time. What "interesting" meant to an investor, he would have made clear to us. At least so I hoped.

"You don't have to be just 'chatter and PowerPoint'."

He looked at us and, for the first time since we had known him, he seemed to come down from the pedestal.

«This world, the world of aspiring startuppers, is full of crap. I see them passing to herds like you; enthusiastic and willing guys, each with a potentially millionaire idea in his head, which he believes is smarter than the others. All dressed in startupper uniforms; your sneakers, your PowerPoint presentations and projections of the future earnings of your startups; think of climbing quickly without realizing that the reality of the market is frictional with the mathematics of your graphs. "

"Is it wrong to want to climb quickly?"

"No, on the contrary, it is mandatory!" he hastened to clarify. «Results divided by time, remember? But I never see one of those projections, where the project is not destined to become

millionaire within the first year; while it usually takes three. 1 They don't realize how much boredom and pressure one has to face between starting a startup and capitalizing it. Ideas crash against boredom: because if there is one true

thing that every self-made man can confirm, it is that getting rich is boring. Have you ever seen one of those movies where the hero trains and there are montages and fades? Well, in real life there are no montages and dissolves: even the small insignificant tasks have to be done and they are the ones that take away the most energy: doing the boring and repetitive details well; the hero does not improve unless he lifts the weights the right number of times, in the right time. Startuppers underestimate this aspect, why they never began to address those points written in their programmatic plan starting from the first; for this reason my advice is to test yourself with a trivial idea, before trying a revolutionary one: to collide with the wall of boredom and have an execution in the historical results to testify your value. "
"Like Jobs with the Mac?"

"Precisely." He opened his briefcase. Inside was an indistinct number of folders. Folders with other folders inside... it makes you think that the last one is also empty.
"What are?"

«People smarter than you. Projects that have passed the first match. It works like this: the first macth serves to get to know each other, to assess whether there is potential. The second serves to confirm or deny that first impression, to understand if the idea really has the potential we thought. The third talks about money and shares ... and eventually agreements are signed like the one that cheated you at the beginning. "

He said it without teasing.

"Courage: choose one, one at random."

We chose a red folder.

"There you have it: programmatic plan. Point one: start of the marketing campaign.

Go on."

"But isn't it confidential material?"

"Yes it is. Are you a reserved type? "

"Yes they are." I understood the game.

He smiled at me and winked at me. «Trust me: there is nothing that has not already been done and thought by someone in these pages. The only one who believes otherwise is the startupper who proposed it to us. "

I read: «Point one: launch of the marketing campaign; point two: business development. Point three: recapitalization of the shares to 300,000 euros ".

«Did you see how fast everything is? In a short time you go from point one to point three and you have already made the first 300,000 euros. "

"Isn't it okay to think quickly?"

"Just think not. Yes, to be. "

"Is it good that I'm fast or not?"

"Of course it's good, you have to be: that's what differentiates you from the others, remember? Your only asset is timing! Reread point one. "

"Point one: launch of the marketing campaign."

"Stop here. You know what that means?"

"Well, I know what a marketing campaign is."

«In their case, it's email marketing: they have to reach six hundred thousand users with a single email; they have the numbers to do it. "

"If they have the numbers, what's the problem?"

«The problem is that they have the numbers on paper! Once I heard a player comment on the prediction data that saw them as favorites: 'On paper we are stronger, it is a pity that we play on grass'. "

"And what does grass consist of in our case?" He handed me the pen and a sheet of paper.

"The grass is that you have six lines to write a message effective enough to convince six hundred thousand people to click on the link that will bring them to us; but first you have to find an object so captivating that it convinces them not to trash it, among the dozens of emails that clog their inbox in the morning."

"Is this my job?"

"No, this is my job. And it's an infinitesimal part of the job. And it usually takes hours."

"To find the right message?"

"Or to find the least wrong: most of the time you do everything in the last ten minutes and then spend the sleepless night rethinking where you should have moved a comma to optimize conversions." 2

"I don't think it sucks, there are those who shovel manure, to live."

"Of course this is heaven for you: it means you are entering the market."

"Not me: I have not yet achieved my execution!"

"Here is my proposal: I offer to be your mentor. 3 In return, I want 10% of your startup, if you make it happen. "

We accepted.

We went into that office in the morning, convinced that 10% was the maximum amount we were willing to sell for a loan of up to 200,000 euros. Now we were giving her away in exchange for advice from a guy we met two hours ago: things change quickly. We offered to pay for breakfast when we took our leave, but he refused: he said that, if we were destined to become partners, then we also had to divide into proportional shares; so we paid the bill and he left the tip.

7.30 pm, in my apartment

When I got home I was unusually tired and excited. I glanced at the inbox, which I hadn't checked for over twenty minutes; reading e-mails on your computer instead of on your phone is like opening the envelope after you peek at it. There were eighteen unread emails: it meant that I had to narrow down a bit more the meshes of my spam filter; while I was basking them, one hit me:

SUBJECT: if I would have known before ...

Who was the illiterate who sent such emails ?! I opened it to laugh some more.

SUBJECT: if I would have known before ...

Here's one thing you won't find in a startupper's programmatic plan: that grammatical error in the subject increases the open rate by 78.2%. If I don't use it for this one, let's remember it for your next campaign; for now it is the best that I have managed to invent.
I am attaching a PDF document, read it before going to bed. And go early. Good execution!
L. Attachment: The True Story of Silicon Valley Parts 1,2,3.

19.36, in my room

I decided to read the attachment lying on the bed. It didn't look like numbers stuff but more like an excerpt from articles taken from a blog: strange he had sent me an attachment instead of a link to a website.

Part 1

I open this post with the idea of telling you how Silicon Valley works, this startup mecca that everyone idolizes as the magical place where things "happen". I hope you read with enthusiasm, because there is very little to enjoy. Know that it is a bluff in the mirror: the things I am about to tell you are absolutely true, you will understand them but you will not want to think that they concern you, you will consider yourself to be the exceptions; it's like that "what weighs more, a kilo of straw or a kilo of lead?" My rational mind knows that, of course, they both weigh a kilo, but part of me doesn't want to believe it and keeps thinking that somewhere there is a one-kilo stack of straw, lighter than a kilo of lead. Well, if you know the history of Silicon Valley and understand how this community has evolved, understand the characteristics of the unique ecosystem in the world that exists here, but let's start from the beginning: Indians and cowboys. Silicon Valley was born like this: so many dreamers in search of gold, few found it and a gentleman, cynical enough, immensely practical and with a particularly concrete business sense, became the richest man in the whole country of the seekers of gold; did he succeed by finding gold? Not at all! He sold shovels and pickaxes ... and in his life he never dug a single gram of earth: it was called Stanford. And since then, nothing has changed: only the way gold is searched has become another, and shovels and picks have been replaced by business plans, market research and PowerPoint slides. Here in Silicon Valley (and wherever one invests in ideas), those who get rich are not so much those who dig, but those who enable the prospector to dig, and this has always been! It was not a metaphor: the first business of this geographical place that today we call Silicon Valley, was really the gold mines. You know Uncle Scrooge in the Klondike? Only it was in California! And lawyer Amasa Leland Stanford, after losing many of his assets in a fire, decided to move there. And he noticed that everyone, absolutely everyone, was looking for gold; so what did he do? Did he go in search of the largest nugget? Not at all! He did the only sensible thing a smart, insightful businessman could do: he opened a shovel and pickaxe shop! Here: Silicon Valley was born in this way, speculating on the dreams of young people in pursuit of their fortune. As I said, nothing has changed since then: just the material the blades are made of! Then it happened that good old Leland became the richest man in Silicon Valley until, one bad day, tuberculosis took his son away; instead of despairing and throwing himself under a train on the railway line (which he had built using Chinese labor, to then make laws against immigration once he entered politics), he decided to found an institute to commemorate him: thus Palo Alto was born and this which we now call Stanford University. This is the origin of that lucky and unrepeatable ecosystem we have here: rich businessmen who have made (more) money by financing young dreamers (an average per capita income, it is said, equal to $ 200,000 each, including children) , research universities that develop technologies and the myth of the hero-entrepreneur who challenges fate e

becomes faber fortunae suae. The games are done, we have served the cards, and Hollywood is ready to consecrate the myth! From all over the world new gold miners are flocking ... but those who really get rich are still those who sell shovels and picks. Be careful, dreamers. To the sellers of broken shovels.

Part 2. The scenario in America today
In the first post I warned you of the dangers of Silicon Valley. Not really: let's say that the post was a warning for all those who cultivate the dream of realizing their business idea and are looking for venture capitalists willing to finance it. I was talking about the cynicism of Silicon Valley and how it all came about from speculators and sifted rivers and a parallel business of shovels, picks and whores ... but I must have been perhaps too cryptic because some of you have commented: "Well, that's not quite the case. ... There are those who have made billions of dollars with an idea ». Ok, in today's post I'll be more explicit.

Point 1. When a new market is born, a series of parallel business opportunities linked to that market are born; and inevitably also a sea of speculators who, on those who dream of making money, want to get rich. Nothing wrong with honest individuals, but the honesty of something also depends on the proportion: and there is no proportion here, believe me, between those who succeed and those who fail. It is a system made to swallow failures: it feeds on ideas that have gone bad and this makes him sick. "That's not true," someone wrote to me, "exception 1" (read Steve Jobs) and "case in a million 2" (for example, the WhatsApp team) made it. True, there are actually quite a few

ridiculous stories built "a posteriori" by excellent storytellers 4 to make the entrepreneurial stories of companies that have had excellent exits poetic and romantic (and therefore more "salable"). Myths to dispel about "the good idea". Mark Zuckerberg, the guys from Google... we all know their stories, right ?! Larry and Sergey made it because they came from Stanford: a mediocre but expensive university, with more connections in the world of ventures than textbooks! Mr. Facebook is said to have stolen the idea from his people

classmates; 5 is not like that, it just outclassed them in the realization and monetization of that idea: here in California they know it very well. If you tell these stories in Silicon Valley they laugh and understand that you are not from there; because here one thing is obvious: how you realize the idea is much more important than the idea itself. Everyone has ideas... I mean, Adams, the inventor of the mouse, after all what did he have on his hands? An innovative technology that had no market: we might as well invent a laser pencil! If Steve Jobs hadn't poked around in the Xerox attic and hadn't "invented" the market for what he took home, today we would probably dictate the lyrics directly into the microphone ... or Google glasses would have been invented earlier, who knows? But these are the stories from the seventies that we all know: they are the myths that inspired us when we were kids... and it doesn't matter, I really mean it, whether you have Bill Gates, Mark Zuckerberg, Larry Page or "Uncle" Jobs in front of your eyes; what you don't know is the Silicon Valley scenario today! Guys: wake up! The venture capitalists you've been chasing have only been slapped in the face for the past decade. Now they are afraid.

Point 2. After Mr. Andreas "Andy" von Bechtolsheim [6] wrote a check

to finance an idea called Google and if it saw it multiplied 360,000 times (the most considerable deal ever done in Silicon

Valley) there was the biggest nerd speculative bubble ever: a real race to finance digital startups; everyone was looking for a "nerd" to stake money on. The result? Over the past decade, venture capitalist investments have yielded an average of 6% ... just over what an average account holder gets! So now there is a lot of fear and the filters have increased. And what happened?

Point 3. The sellers of shovels and picks have multiplied! Offices designed for coworking, where you pay to stay, pay to meet financiers, sell shares to meet consultants who you will then pay to introduce you to someone who matters... now gold must be looked for elsewhere, listen to me. Smell the Valley, but go back while you are in time; Fortune is sought when there is no mass: when the whole world knows about your deposit, it is no longer time to dig, it is time to sell! To the good connoisseur ...

Part 3. Get out of the startup trap!
This article concludes a trilogy of posts about Silicon Valley that I have decided to title "The Whole Truth About SV". Judging by your comments, the topic touched you

a lot. Since I suggested that we go and seek our fortune elsewhere, e
since you have all read the tale of the Alchemist, 7 today I will dedicate myself to the Italian scenario. It seems that Plug & Play, the giant of exit strategies, which dealt with the acquisition of PayPal by eBay so to speak, wants to open an office in Italy, and you are all in turmoil ... I understand you but I fear more for the damage than yes they can do; I will try to explain myself, and I swear it will be the last time, then this blog closes.

We assume that no one invests large amounts without having control; in Silicon Valley, for example, there is an 80-mile rule: if you want my money you have to open up here, get on a spit and get checked out. In addition, the lawyer, the accountant, the tax advisor and all your consultants must be here, preferably my trusted men; Silicon Valley is like the moon: it's another planet. And oh well, the moon is a satellite, but we don't formalize ourselves. You can't hire a Mars lawyer to do business on Saturn, and that seems pretty obvious to me... but any place where ideas are funded is a planet unto itself; if you are in Rome, take a Roman lawyer: and choose a divorce, if what you have to face is a divorce! But I'm digressing ... what I want to tell you is:

You have to get out of the trap of this world that wants you to startupper for life
and start thinking about it a little less startuppers and a little more entrepreneurs!

Having an idea is nothing! Making it happen is already something, but knowing how to turn it into a business is EVERYTHING, believe me! Do you think I don't see you at conferences? That you don't meet at conferences? They are parties: that's all. These "startup weekends" 8 of which all
you seem to go crazy are circus wagons: as useful to your projects as the Motor
Show is useful for those who want to buy a car! They are huge construction sites that advertise shovel & pickaxe sellers! Stop! Detoxify! Get out of the startup tunnel!

Are you looking for lenders for your idea? Instead, you start by assuming that NO ONE will ever give you a euro: what do you do in that case? Is it still a brilliant idea? Will you spend your life drinking at the bar, complaining that "if I was born in Ammeriga I would be a millionaire by now" ?!

But we will not understand this before we see deaths on the street and people who get seriously hurt, both from the startupper side and from the investor side; because we are Italian, we want to "possess", not "participate". We prefer to become the masters of an amateur team, rather than remain the bench in a noble Serie A team.

Moral of the story: here we want to be "more American than Americans" without the means to do so; I still have to see a million euro exit that was not exported and made elsewhere, before being sold. Yet everyone wants to start up! We brought shovels and picks, but we forgot to export the fields and mines as well. On the other hand, we have a lot of consultants and a lot of chatter on the subject ... Listen to me: get out of the startup trap! More than in Silicon Valley it feels like being in Hollywood, where everyone claims to be actors, but everyone works in a different restaurant! Startuppers who do not quickly become entrepreneurs remain aspiring! What you have to do, if you really intend to build your startup, is to get out of this trap that wants you to start up for life! Establish your company, create it lean and dynamic, make it work even if no one will finance you: because no one will finance you! It's statistics: everyone buys scratch cards but no one would dream of really planning investments on their future hoping to find the winning ticket. So abandon the addiction to ventures, because here in Italy there are none!

The most you will find is a modest loan of a few tens of thousands of euros, for a large part of the company; and you will both take the rip-off, because there have been very few exits worthy of the name in Italy so far. Peace and good business.

THE BUSINESS ARTIST

Evolution of investments and speculative bubbles in Silicon Valley.

Lesson n. 3

Execution matters much more than the idea, the creative potential, the contacts and the money you have.
Execution is what lenders invest in.

Venture capitalists do not finance a potential idea or a half-completed project: they finance the execution that you have proven you can do up to now.
Your idea doesn't matter, your execution counts.
Execution has reasonable results in an interesting time frame. to
a Interesting means short: the faster you are, the more interesting you become. My only asset is timing!

1   To avoid this criticism, today's strategy is to draw up business plans in which the idea monetizes in the third year, to make them credible: however, having also become a standard, it does not help. My advice is: write business plans that monetize when you really think you can monetize.

2   Optimizing conversions is technical jargon: by conversion we mean the passage from a state A to a state B. For example, a potential customer who, through our intervention, becomes an effective customer. In this case the expression is used to indicate the transition from users who receive the email to users who read it and click on it. Since those who carry out these

operations keep a statistical average of the results, optimizing means improving that average.

3   A mentor is one who has been through this before. He has knowledge, contacts and skills.

4   Storytelling is a branch of copywriting that has the function of creating pleasant stories to spread in order to make them "viral". The typical example is the alleged birth of Apple in a garage: all the companies of that time were born in garages or basements but only the Cupertino company made it a flag. The same goes for Jobs 'proverbial fussiness or for Bill Gates' negotiation with IBM during which the license for the MS-DOS was negotiated: the "legend" (or viral story to be precise) he wants Gates, after the negotiation, without a program even in the slightestsimilar to what he had just "sold", he rushed to buy a "system operating disk" (abbreviated DOS) from another company and then modify it and pass it off as his own (the initial MS-DOS acronym stands for " Microsoft ").

5   The famous film The Social Network focuses its plot precisely on the lawsuit that ensued.

6   Co-founder of Sun Microsystem; legend has it that the name Google is due to him. So declares Sergey Brin: "We met very early one morning in Palo Alto on the steps of the home of a Stanford faculty member. We showed him a quick demo. He was in a hurry, had other appointments, and said, 'Instead of discussing all the details, why don't I write you a check right away?' It was registered to Google Inc. and it was for $ 100,000. " (In fact, Bechtolsheim's was the initial funding and that amount was fundamental to laying the first brick that allowed the company to quickly reach the million dollars to complete the fundraising.) However, there being no company with that name, the check lay in a drawer of Larry Page's desk for weeks, until in September 1998, aMenlo Park, California, the company was born. For the record: Larry Page opened the doors of their first offices with a remote control. They were in fact located in the car shed that a friend sublet to the company. As you can see, even Google was born in a garage!

7   Famous Arab story, made famous by the homonymous book by Paulo Coelho, in which the protagonist leaves

the house in search of a treasure only to discover that it was buried in his garden.
8   Seminars dedicated to startups and their creation and / or presentation.

Lesson n. 4. Business model

Starting a company does NOT mean starting a startup!
8 March - 8.00 am, mentor's office

Our mentor had had to leave for a week for urgent work commitments and we had counted the days hoping that he had not forgotten us or had not set us aside for a more interesting project. When we met him again, he did not disappoint: we found him focused, and he had even done research "on the piece".
«Ok, you want to do a startup; let's start with the basics: do you know the difference between a company and a startup? "
"Of course."
"Tell me."
"A startup is a company in its infancy."
He looked at me as if I had kicked the penalty of victory in the wrong door, then he took his head in his hands, in despair. It had taken six months to organize our first match, it started in the worst way and finished in minutes. And now the arrogant and slightly older guy who had sent him to the winds was asking us the

easiest of questions ... and I couldn't answer!
"No problem," he said, rousing himself. "It's all normal, aspiring startuppers don't worry about practical things: they prefer to go to Google to contemplate the potential of their idea instead of studying how the tool with which they intend to make it works works." He consoled himself more than me. "Simple simple definition, but a little less simple than Wikipedia ..." and wrote:

A company is a company.

So far we were there.

A startup is a temporary business association, formed with the aim of creating a repeatable, scalable and profitable business model.

"What strikes you most about this definition?"
"The word 'temporary'."
"True: it suggests the concept of timing ..." he added.
"Our only asset!" I hastened to clarify.

"Until you have a expendable execution, in fact. Copy this definition in your notes, exactly as it is written. "
We ran.
"Now learn it by heart: later I will ask you to repeat it to me." We were back in elementary school.

«What you need to understand is that timing and execution are important for both companies and startups; but for startuppers the rules are much more complicated: the doors are narrower. "
"Tighter?"
"What I mean," he explained, looking us straight in the eye, "is that you don't start a startup to work on it. Companies start with the intention of starting something, maybe building a business; sometimes they are even born as a family business: when you start your own business or set up a company, your ambition may very well be to get to invoice a figure with which to cover costs and earn profits that give some satisfaction. "
"And isn't this also the intent of a startup? Producing profits ?! "
"It is too simplistic a vision: the startup was not born to get by, it was born to explode or die."

"What do you mean by dying?"

"I mean you have to give yourself a time in which to succeed or give up; if you don't, the lenders will give it to you anyway: if the idea doesn't work, the same person who helped you bring it to light will turn it off without the right of appeal and you won't be able to do anything to prevent it. "

"You mean the lender is going to sell off the company?"

"Exact. After receiving a loan, you will have a very limited time to grow everything quickly and pay back the investment will not be enough: venture capitalists invest on risk and simply returning the amount does not satisfy them, they want to multiply. "

"But I don't understand: if our startup is healthy ..."

"That it is healthy is not enough: it must burst with health otherwise it will end up like a lame horse." As he said this, he made the gun gesture to his temple.

"Is that why venture capitalists give money to those who bring results quickly?"

"Exact. The money you will receive will help you go faster, but you will not receive any more if you do not know how to grow as they expect from you; and this is the trickiest part, not receiving the money: when they finance you, you will no longer have control and you will depend on other people. And at any time, those people can decide whether to draw a check for fuel ... or the plug on the car that keeps you alive, sell off everything and bet on another horse. "

It was a perspective that we had never considered: until now we had only puzzled over where to find the means to carry out our project, but we had never asked ourselves the question of how to proceed once it was done. This is the most important difference between a company and a startup: the company can afford to have ups and downs, to survive and proceed slowly, to remain stable for a while. A startup can only grow suddenly or be canceled: the time available was limited; those two words - timing and execution - were becoming my obsession. Our mentor saw the despair in my eyes and seemed to rush to my aid.

"Now don't think about it, let's go to lunch: later I'll explain how to avoid being sold off by the financiers." I nodded unconvinced.

Lesson n. 4 (continued)

A startup and a company are two different things.
A startup must be: repeatable, scalable, profitable.
The company was born to grow; the startup was born to scale and move beyond.

End-of-level monsters
1.30 pm, (non) working lunch

We didn't talk about work at lunch. I tried to slip the subject here and there, but our mentor was shy: "At lunch we have lunch," he said. "Don't underestimate the value of a break." However, he had gone out to talk on his cell phone two or three times during the meal, a sign that even he couldn't keep some business waiting. Only when the coffee arrived did he pull out his diary and asked us: "Is the idea a good one?"
"Yup."
"On what basis are you saying it?"
"I feel that."
"Let's see if your instincts are right; refresh my memory: what is a startup? "
This time I knew the answer:

A startup is a temporary business association, formed with the aim of creating a repeatable, scalable and profitable business model.

«Exactly, and it is on these three words that you decide whether your project has value or not. Everyone has an idea: some even manage to make it happen. But both the idea and the way it is made must respect these three parameters:

Repeatable - Scalable - Profitable

"Consider them three doors through which to pass ... three conditions to be met: both your idea and your business model must pass these three tests."
He wrote on the board:

Be repeatable. Be scalable. Be profitable.

«Since you are young, imagine it as if it were a video game: to free the princess (that is, to create your startup) you have to overcome three monsters at the end of the level. At the first level you will find a monster called Repeatability: to beat it you have to show that your business can be repeated and that it is not too tied to a

current fashion or temporary conditions. He is an easy monster to beat, as in all video games at the first level.

MONSTER TO BEAT LEVEL 1
Repeatable business.

"The second level is presided over by a slightly stronger monster called Scalability. To beat it, your business needs to be not only repeatable, but also scalable, meaning that you can go from one customer to one hundred thousand customers or even millions of customers, without requiring too much effort for you. This monster is tough, but never like the one you'll face if you get through it.

MONSTER TO BEAT LEVEL 2
Scalable business.

"On the third level of our game there is an even more difficult monster, which is the worst of all, and it's called Profitability. Your business has to monetize, that is, it has to carry money in your pockets. It is the most difficult monster, because it seems the simplest, but it is not: making a profit is not as obvious as you may think. Let's try to play. "

MONSTER TO BEAT LEVEL 3
Monetizable business.

He armed us with paper, pen, and everything needed to take notes. We looked like nerds playing Dungeons & Dragons, 1 but we were something else.
«This is how you evaluate whether an idea is good or not: to be good, it must respect i
parameters of the startup that we are going to build around us. So it must embody the three characteristics you now know by heart. "
"Repeatable, scalable and profitable ..."
«Precisely: let's start with the first. Can you explain again what repeatable means? "
"I think so. Repeatable means that it must be able to be reproduced over time. "
«Put simply: it is not enough for a single deal to be concluded once or only under certain market conditions; To be solid, our business must stand up in all scenarios and must be able to repeat itself over time. This is the obvious part, let's

delve into the concept with slightly less obvious questions. Is your business repeatable? And in what way? Is it everywhere? In any condition? Will it last over time? Is it related to a fashion? Is it valid for the whole year? "

He explained to us that there are "timed" businesses designed to last a couple of years and then become extinct, exploiting a trend and a peak. He represented them on a Gaussian curve. 2 It was interesting, but it wasn't our case: our business surpassed the first monster

level: it was repeatable!

"Now we come to the second condition ..."

"Scalable."

«It means that our business model must be able to be reproduced to scale without

that this poses a problem for us. For example, a restaurant focused on the skill of the chef, where only one man is the star product, is not scalable; on the contrary, the McDonald's restaurant chain is. You have to make your business as little dependent as possible on talent, yours but also others'. You don't have to rely on key people but on key procedures. The question is, can you cope with exponential growth? Going from one customer to 100,000 customers seamlessly? I'll give you some examples. Let's say our business is to sell books: how can we go from 10,000 copies to 100,000 overnight? Answer: by selling ebooks. Another example: lessons. How can we go from 10 students to 500? Classroom course. And 5,000? "

"We could... hold webinars." 3

"Perfect. But let's stay on the 'physical' because with the software it is too easy to satisfy the scalability criterion. Imagine having a family business for generations in the food & beverage market, let's say an ice cream parlor. Imagine having dreams of glory and ambition and wanting to create a chain of ice cream shops with your brand. Now you have a problem: ice cream, as good as you make it, is the result of your experience of generations and generations, which cannot be transferred quickly. In addition, the ingredients, on which quality largely depends, you always find fresh because for years you have been served by the same suppliers: but you cannot guarantee the same quality for the other points you open. What are you doing to solve this problem? "

"Well ... shall we lower the quality and focus everything on marketing?"

«Exactly: but you cannot suddenly lower the quality of the ice cream after you have accustomed your customers to a certain standard: the quality of your product must immediately be that. And then perhaps it is better to think this way from the beginning: first create the need to scale and find the solutions to do it before entering the market. "

"Do not replicate the family business as it is, but find other characteristics?"

«You should create a new concept that people can appreciate: not focus, as everyone does, on quality, but emphasize another immediately recognizable characteristic. Maybe the dispensing of ice cream different from any other, or the possibility of customizing it as desired using ingredients that are not found elsewhere! "

To recap: it was not easy, but it was essential to start with it clear from the beginning that the purpose of the game, that is, of the business, was exponential growth; that is to say climb. A family-run business was not created, at least not anymore, in the era that saw the internet on one side and the economic recession on the other. If we had created a company for the purpose of working within it, no one would have ever considered us, nor would we have ever become entrepreneurs. By following this strategy we could at most aim to become good craftsmen or professionals: whoever did not create a company to resell it aiming to capitalize millions of euros, was not a startupper, he was a manager! As I mentally reviewed the lesson, the mentor was preparing to conclude:

«You don't climb by pure luck, just as you don't participate in the Olympics by luck: you prepare and study, there is specific training and actions to be taken. First we will deal with the design, and it is that 'thinking big' that will get us through the three levels; but it is also important to climb for another reason: if you have a partner

who gave you 100 or 200 kappa 4 to go, won't settle for a company that gets by. By getting by, we obviously intend to make 50% of the investment within two or three years. The accounts do not add up: because venture capitalists work on gambling (venture, precisely) so they do not want to contain the damage, they want to fail loudly or just as loudly explode. A success must be explosive, or it is not a success: climb quickly or abandon the project! " He paused for a while and concluded: "Are there any questions?"

"One thing is not clear to me ..."

"You are welcome."

"In your example with there ice cream parlor, we had already an activity: not Could we simply expand it and change the marketing strategy as we go about it? "

"Sure, but it would be extremely risky, because you would lose the timing."

"I understand ... it is easier to start from scratch than to correct during construction."

«Do you see how it was already much more difficult to satisfy the second parameter than the first? Now we come to the third ingredient. "

"Profitable."

"This is a fundamental concept: what allows you to monetize an idea?"

"Er ... the fact that it makes money ?!"

«It would seem obvious but in fact it is not that easy; many startups were funded before they even made money: we have already talked about the most famous of

these: Google, remember? The ventures did not know how it could make a profit at the time of financing, they only made it possible for Larry Page and Sergey Brin to be joined by a director of proven value, that is to say that ... "
"Did he have a spendable execution behind him ?!"
"Correct."
"So what does that 'monetizable' consist of? How could Google be if it didn't generate money? "
"Do you know what those who want to make money but can't find the right way to make money have to worry about?"
"We wouldn't be here if we knew ..."
"Find a way to help as many people as possible."
"Becoming like Mother Teresa?"
"If you mean the saint of Calcutta, know that at her death the foundation that bears her name had assets worth billions of euros, but I am not referring exactly to this; what makes a startup profitable is the answer to these two questions. " He stopped talking and wrote:

QUESTION No. 1
What problem does it solve?

QUESTION No. 2
How many have that problem?

«A startup must solve a problem: if there is no problem, there is no profit. And that problem must be widespread: the more widespread it is, the more money we will make. "

"I'm not following you: what problem does Google solve?"
"Could you tell me who finished second in the athletics competition at the 2008 Olympics, in which cinema they make Scorsese's last film and how far is London airport from the City?"
"No I do not know."
"And if you need to know the answers, if it was a matter of life or death, or if you just paid yourself to tell me, would you be able to find that information in ten minutes?"
"Well, yes, it would be enough to go to G ..."
"70 million searches are made every minute on Google: who did we ask all those questions to before ?!"
I was beginning to understand: money was not necessarily the central point, but the consequence of the business model; if around the idea, any idea, it was possible

to create a mechanism capable of functioning as a system, and if that system was at the same time reproducible, replicable and able to serve many people, then the business model could work regardless of the idea. Once we thought of a business model based on those factors, we proceeded with the execution, trying to obtain reasonable results in an interesting time; and if it worked, the venture capitalist would inject massive amounts of money to scale as quickly as possible ...

«As in any video game, often to beat the monster of a particularly difficult level our player must evolve. In this case, evolving means identifying the key to correctly interpreting the question. And the key to getting through the third level is that we need to stop thinking about the idea and start focusing on the business model. "

"The business model," I repeated thoughtfully.

"Exact. If the idea is repeatable and scalable then it's good, but for the startup we will create to make that idea work, we need a third factor to be added ... "

"Could it be profitable ?!"

"Precisely. And when we talk about profit we are no longer talking about the idea: we are talking about a model, that is a scheme with simple steps, which will allow us to do. "
"Meaning the business model?"
"Yup. The business model can be summarized in a question:

How do we make money?

"So now I ask you: how do we make money?"
"Well, it's basically an app, so I would say from advertising ... or we could charge a euro to each person who downloads it ... or even give a free version and charge the premium version ..."
«As you can see, it is not at all easy to answer. We have a thousand options and models to choose from, and we don't know which one could be the best. "
"So?"

"So we'll start with the basics; since September 1998, if you have a startup you can have it of two types: digital or traditional. Personally, I love traditional startups because ... "
"What happened in September 1998?"

"Google was founded: the $ 100,000 investment to found the company paid off   times; an unprecedented record; for a while everyone wanted to invest in digital startups: fashion started and the bloodbaths began... Didn't you read the attachment to the email I sent you? "

"Yes, but this detail escaped me."

"A little bad. Personally, I said, I love traditional startups because they are real things, which you can touch: there is little philosophy and you will hardly find the far-fetched projections of some students on how 'within three years the 1% we are giving you will be worth 2 million euro 'and blah blah blah. Don't get me wrong: those blah blah blah are important and you have to learn to tell them well, but not to argue with who has to give you real money ... with those you have to use another language that I will teach you to speak. Traditional startups need sold contracts and services provided: consider me a dinosaur, after all I am over thirty years old and you are kids, but I grew up in the middle of the street and I used up the soles of my shoes selling door to door, so this is a world that I know and that I can control.

"The question is: if traditional businesses need transactions, what do digital ones need?"

"I don't know ... customers ?!"

"Precisely! The customers of physical companies are calculated on the basis of the contracts signed, while for digital startups the key word is population. " He crossed out the question marks and completed the pattern:

"Population," I repeated in a low voice.

«Do you know the companies Facebook, Instagram and WhatsApp? You know what the value is
intrinsic to those former startups? "

"Of course we know them and, yes: not in detail but I'd say billions of dollars ..."

"Do you know why all these companies are worth billions of dollars?"

"Why ... do they generate high turnover and decent margins?"

"In part, yes, but that's not the only reason they are worth so much. Do you really believe that Facebook bills even a tenth of the money it is worth? No, these companies are not worth the money they make, but they are worth the money they make! And even more so for what they potentially do. "

"Is that why they went public?"

«But the stock exchange is only the instrument that allows you to exchange the value of those shares and fix their price; and I highly doubt that two inexperienced guys like you know the magic of stock indices, so no, the question I'm asking is simpler and more important: what made venture capitalists decide that Facebook had enormous potential? "

"The number of people involved?"

"Exact! What you need to understand is that it doesn't matter whether you buy on the internet or not: the moment you interact through the web, you become a potential consumer. And every time you are interested in something it is as if you were looking at a shop window: those companies sell you, or rather, they sell to other companies the information you have just seen in that showcase ... This is what the business is based on: place a photo of your daughter and you become a potential consumer for a diaper company... user information, this is the market; moreover, the more and better the user interacts, the better and more reliable the information you can 'sell'. "

I was beginning to understand the game; I resumed the scheme and circled the object of our focus:

"Take the case of Instagram: a free application that earned practically nothing, but what did it possess of great value?"
"Population?"
«That's right: more than 200 million users and exclusive information. Furthermore, it could only be used on the iPhone; this immediately created a strong sense of desire for those who owned Android phones and a sense of exclusivity for Apple users. "
"Risky..."
"But brilliant: it was the main reason it was sold to Facebook for the figure

disproportionate to a billion dollars, and after only two years; they carried out the transaction at the moment of greatest interest, that is to say in conjunction with the launch of the Android version and the listing of Facebook on the stock exchange. All while Google launched its Google Plus, which further expanded the photosharing market. "

"Brilliant of course, but also very, very lucky!"

«Luck favors prepared minds: do you know what Picasso said? 'When inspiration comes, he'll find me there painting.' "

«Are you talking about inspiration ?! Just you who are the man of numbers? "

«Replace 'inspiration' with 'market opportunity' and you will have the formula to have luck with our startup. If you choose to create a digital startup, know that almost all of those born today crash against the population wall. Let me explain it even better:

Population
=
How many people use it regularly.

«It doesn't matter that your product is the best, it matters how many users actually use it. And I'm not talking about how many have it: but how many users are happy to use it often. Every idea, every application, every software and service, is useless if there are not every day users happy to use it often and willingly. "

"Think of Microsoft, of Google. Think YouTube! " He closed his laptop and displayed the apple logo. "Do you really think it matters that Macs look better and perform better than PCs?" Most people won't switch to Mac anyway because people are too lazy to switch to a simpler operating system. They struggle to think different, even if that different makes their life easier! Most people resist change. Look at this image: do you know it? " he asked, and opened a slide on his computer:

"Sure, it's from Seth Godin's The Purple Cow."
"Exact. But the design is disproportionate, that's how it should be. " He clicked on the button and a new screen appeared:

"Seth Godin's pessimism is more than optimistic! Or at least that's how we should think of it because I assure you that things will be much more difficult than you imagine! Do you remember the mailing campaign of the red folder? "
"Yes, your email with the grammatical oversight ... brilliant!"
"It's proceeding slowly. If something doesn't change, the project won't see the light. "

"I understand ... on paper it was brilliant, too bad you play on the grass."
«Never mind: it's your project that you have to be interested in. Is everything clear up to now? "
"Crystalline."
"Well! So since ours is a digital start-up, we are concerned with population: attracting the minimum number of users to reach the break even point will be our reasonable result to be achieved in an interesting time. "
"What strategy will we adopt to succeed?"
"This question is about the how; how we will deal with when we move on to execution: you still do not have clear all the steps to take. And with this we say goodbye for today. "

Lesson n. 4 (continued)

In order not to die before being born, your startup must be:
to. Repeatable
b. Scalable
c. Profitable. to
a Profitable does not necessarily have to do with money (at least in this first phase), for example, for digital startups the key word is population.

Serial failures
12 March - 1.00 pm, mentor's office

We had been working on the business model for a few days now, in what had become our second office, namely the mentor's room. "I like how you are putting my advice into practice. We will soon take the first step, so we have to make one thing clear right away. "
"What do you mean?"
"You are doomed to fail."
We looked at it as the first time he took our project apart.
"We ... will we fail?"
"Definitely."
"But ... the business model works."
"I think so too. Nevertheless, you will fail. "
"Why?! I mean ... tell us why and let's see how we can avoid it! "
"It would be a bad approach: the most wrong of all!"
"I do not understand."
"This is the main reason why you haven't done anything to date: you want to avoid failure."
"Explain better ..."

"Imagine walking into a club and noticing a girl you like." I nodded: it wasn't very difficult to imagine.

"You would like to try an approach, but you are hesitant because you are afraid of receiving rejection."

I nodded again: it was an extremely common scene for me.

"And what's the best way not to hit the two of spades?" I knew the answer.

"Don't even try: stay glued to the bar stool." I remained silent.

"After a while, someone will come and blow the girl from you: this is what happens to those who want to avoid failure."

I felt caught in a nutshell: in two words he had exactly described my sentimental situation and my awkwardness with women.

"I see you're not saying anything, is this situation familiar to you?" I nodded in agreement.

"The real question is: who taught you to behave this way?"

"Nobody ... I'm like that ... I'm shy."

"You weren't as a child."

"How can you tell?"

«Nobody is born shy. Put two children who do not know each other in a room -

they will take a few seconds to make friends. Instead, he puts two adults in the elevator: they read and reread the cursed plate with maximum capacity and capacity for ten floors until they memorize it, so as not to speak ... Who taught us that? "
"The life?"

"Do you remember the list of your classmates? That's where it all started... "He was obsessed with school!
«Teachers pass on useful information, but they do it the wrong way: they teach how to avoid mistakes! Today's school is anachronistic: it does not encourage dialogue between colleagues, creative problem solving, stealing the solution with one's eyes ... "
I smiled, thinking of all the times I had tried to steal the solution to the task with my eyes.
«But what is worse, at school they teach to avoid mistakes: to do a task well you have to do it without mistakes; the professor circles the errors with a red pen ... so what do you learn? To try to avoid mistakes! What they should teach instead is the right way to make mistakes! "
"Is there a right way?"

"Of course yes: I wouldn't be here if I hadn't made mistakes." He was extremely serious.

"Well, neither do we." And I thought about how I had messed up the meeting with the investor and how our relationship was born from this.

"You have to know two things about mistakes; the first is that ... "he broke off and wrote:

A single mistake doesn't kill.

"A single mistake doesn't kill ..." I repeated.

"I'm not done," the mentor pointed out, completing the sentence:

A single mistake doesn't kill. The sum of more mistakes kills.

"Take any news story: from the Titanic tragedy to a fight in a bar. You will find that it is not the single mistake that has determined the tragedy, but the sum of several mistakes. It is never the glance or the word too many, it is the glances followed by the words too many that ignite the fuse. Conversely, when the error is single it does not necessarily lead to a disadvantage. Take your case: presenting yourself from the venture with just the idea was a mistake; you had this clear from the first day and it is the first thing we said to each other, however look at that mistake where it led you: if you had not committed it, you would still be presenting the NDA in vain. No error is irreparable, what is irreparable is the sum of several errors. It's like a game of chess: sometimes you have to give up on recovering a lost piece, if, on the other hand, you continue to defend a desperate position, you risk losing the game. The important thing is to learn from every mistake: you could have chosen to leave, instead you shared the idea and invested in timing; you put that mistake to good use and turned it into a competitive advantage, that's good! When you make a mistake, what you have to avoid is to behave like a fly: never learn from mistakes. "

"A fly?"

«It often happens that flies manage to enter through a crack in a door and then no longer manage to get out of an apparently wide open window; Have you ever seen a fly fly to freedom and hit the glass of a window? "

I nodded.
"But the flies are stubborn: the insect tries again, with more running, falls again, gets up and starts again."
"They are stubborn: isn't that good for a startupper?"
«Stubbornness is good, but only if between the moment you fall and the moment you get up you give yourself time to learn something: gaining more motivational momentum without studying a different strategy is what kills the flies; have you ever seen them dead on the windowsill? "
I nodded again.
"The glass didn't kill them, it killed them the repeated mistake without learning anything from the previous one: don't be like the fly!"
I was beginning to understand.
"And yet, you don't have to avoid bankruptcy at any cost either, because that's what has prevented you from bringing home any concrete result up to now!"
"But we're at the beginning!" I protested.

"It is not a good reason not to immediately start accumulating dozens and dozens of mistakes and a couple of good hits to put on the bench; and that's the only thing that will set you apart from the crowd. What have you done so far to distinguish yourself from the thousand hungry and ballsy kids out there, apart from the chatter? "

We had no tangible result to argue with, so we remained silent.

"Remember one thing: Investors don't look kindly on two types of people: those who do everything themselves and those who don't have bankruptcy behind them."

"I mean ... failure is okay too, as long as we don't stand still?"

"Have you ever heard: 'You are not credible if you have not failed at least three times'?"

"Yes, I've heard it ... but this is true in other places: in these parts an entrepreneur who fails is branded for life."

The mentor burst out laughing. «Fail... branded for life. Oh my God, this is the first time I've heard it! " He wasn't kidding: he was really falling apart. «My friend: there is a way and a way to fail... I certainly did not mean bankruptcy! I'm not saying that your company should go bankrupt or be a commissioner: that doesn't exclude you from the game, but it's certainly not a good business card! "

I was confused: what exactly did he mean then, when he said fail? He smiled and pointed to an open frame hanging on the wall. It contained a photocopy of a faded check.

«Ok, let's clarify what is meant by failure in startup jargon. That was one of my first failures: a company that should have dominated the renewable energy market, but which after just a year and a half failed miserably! "

"What was the problem?"

«Difference of views on managerial management. Or rather, this was the official version; the real reason was that the commercial director we had put in charge of the network was a scammer who was stealing money from the company's coffers, but we never managed to prove it and in the end he set me and my partner against the entire board of directors . He was very smart, even if incorrect: a real thoroughbred horse, too bad he was a thief! "

"What happened to the company?"

"Oh, it's still standing as far as I know, even though it never took off; we were forced to sell our shares ... "

"Was it a hard blow?"

«Well, what do I have to tell you ... we believed in it a lot and we had committed eighteen months of our life to that project; in the end we were forced to sell our majority shares for around 200,000 euros. "

"How!? 200,000 euros for eighteen months of work, do you call it a failure? "

"Well, it's all relative: we didn't want to sell and we expected to earn a lot more ... and then we had contracted debts: that money was used to cover a part of it."

"And how much did you put in your pocket?"

"About 90,000 euros for couples."

"Still not bad for a year and a half of work."

"As a consultant I could earn a lot more and without entrepreneurial risks."

"Why don't you do it then?"

«Because when there are risks, there are also opportunities! I mean, in more than one project I have risked not earning anything and even going at a loss, but I have also come close to a millionaire exit a couple of times. "

In fact it was true, we were informed and the term "touched" was an understatement. "No risk, no gain, huh?"
«Security and freedom do not mix: deal with it! The question is just how many times will you be able to get up after falling. If the answer is: 'One more time', you are already halfway there ... "he smiled," the other half is not acting like the fly! " Then he added: "I will not tell you to look at the glass half full, but know that this is how most people relate to success, their own or others."
With his pen he drew a pattern:

"And that's the way things actually go." He sketched a second diagram alongside the first:

BANKRUPTCY → BANKRUPTCY → BANKRUPTCY → SUCCESS

"And this is why they do nothing: they want to avoid bankruptcy at all costs and they fail before they even begin; while that's how things really go. "
"If you are aware of this situation and, despite everything, you have the strength to get involved and get up again, you have already won."

"Doesn't luck count?" I asked.
«Of course it matters, it also takes luck. But luck is a skill that trains. "
"How do you train your luck?"
He became serious all of a sudden. "I don't want to lie to you: while you fail and immediately after, when you hit rock bottom and are defenseless, in those moments they will have no mercy on you: you will

all against; the competitors who did the same thing, the opponents who did the exact opposite, and especially the opportunists who did nothing: all ready to hit you where it hurts the most. But just as there is no place in the world where you will be safe from jackals, there is no place in the world where those who have tried, failed and got up are not considered a reliable and experienced person by those who make things happen. what's this."
"That is, who finances your execution."
«Exactly, because it means that you have shown that you can face failure and start again; and to do this it takes character. You have shown that you have skills. "

Lesson n. 4 (continued)

Success involves a series of countless failures. Failing does not mean declaring bankruptcy.
Security and freedom do not go together.
It is true that "It doesn't matter how many times you fall, but how many you get up", however "Don't be like the fly!"

Step by step
2.59 pm, agenda: we are still at the business model ... and I urgently need a coffee
"Can we take a break?"
"You are tired?"
"I'd give 2% for a cup of coffee!"
"Then no break: under stress, the best ideas are born."
"But ... at lunch you said not to underestimate the breaks."
"And I was right: now you're tired because you didn't switch off when you had to, next time learn from me."
"But you were phoning while ..." It was useless, he was no longer listening to me.
"Let's start over: is the idea a good one?"
"It is." I said it and I was convinced of it.
"On what basis are you saying it?"
"Well, it's repeatable, scalable, and profitable."

"I agree: and this time, instinct is not involved, you say that the idea is good because you have carried out an analysis." It was true and I knew it. But it wasn't just that: the idea had actually evolved. "To tell the truth, the idea we have now is no longer the original one."

"And what has changed since then?"

«By adapting the idea to the parameters you gave us, that idea has improved: now it is no longer an intuition, but a real project. I would say the biggest difference is this: thinking in terms of repeatable, scalable and profitable has changed everything. Now it's really more solid! "

"It is because you started thinking like a startupper, rather than a fool who shows up with an NDA at the first meeting."

"Will you never stop reminding me?"

"No, because I don't want you to make such a mistake again. And also because, when you are about to get millions from the exit of your startup, it is good that you remember who brought you there. " He smiled but I still thought that part of him wasn't joking at all.

«Now I ask you again: on the basis of these three characteristics the idea is really good? "

"It is." I was increasingly convinced of it.

«This is enough for me. Personally, I am very little interested in the idea: I jump directly to the next point, after all ... "

Here, finished: with this the first point is evaded. Is the idea good? You like it? Well! It mattered little to our mentor. What mattered to him was that the business model stood up. But what struck me was that I was starting to think like him, so I cut him off. "I guess you're going to say, 'If the business model works and the team is there, the idea may not be that great.'

My mentor smiled. "You don't put the idea at the center anymore, I'm pleased with that."

«I understood that the greatest risk one runs when designing a startup is to fall in love with the idea; when you get too attached to the idea, stop thinking as entrepreneurs and make mistakes, startups are born to break away from it: it's like raising a child: sooner or later you have to let it run on its own legs, otherwise it never becomes an adult. We've definitely talked about the idea too much. "

"If you really understand all of this, we can begin to get serious."

"Weren't we already doing it?"

The mentor laughed. «Do you really think that those few arguments were a beginning of work ?! Do you think companies design themselves on a paper napkin? "
"Well ... I'd like to think so."
«And so it is, but then you have to get the deck! And now let's start planning seriously: I'll show you the steps to take. " Having said that, our mentor drew a pattern:

"That is to say we come up with the idea, face the monsters and go through the three levels, that is, we create a business model that works, we execute our execution, we get funded, we scale as quickly as possible and we sell everything! Here are the phases of the process: from here on we will think about our startup having as guidelines the steps of this scheme. The good news is that the first point, namely the idea, we have evaded; and on the second we are well on the way, because it passed the scalability and repeatability criteria. We are on the right track as to whether it can be monetized, a criterion that calls into

question the prospects for earnings. The rest is up to you: I have opened a folder in Dropbox with some material to complete and will upload more as we proceed. It will be your homework. "
We nodded.
"I guess you already know Dropbox."
"Yup."
«Their startup was financed by creating a beta version of the project for demonstration purposes and proposing the idea to users; a sort of social focus group 5; the extraordinary number of users who declared their interest in the project convinced the ventures
capitalist to finance the startup. "
«I understand: the number of 'likes' was their execution; the useful result in interesting times. "
"Exact. And speaking of results, by 10 am tomorrow morning I expect the complete job: let's see if your business model is right too. " We were finally there! The much-proclaimed execution: it was our turn to produce results!

FROM THE SHARED FOLDER IN DROPBOX
Business Model Canvas

Dear guys, I leave you this scheme to use to think about your business model: it is the Canvas Model. Its creator, Alexander Osterwalder, put it on
available on the network. 6 To use it effectively, all you have to do is print it and attach it to the wall: I spent several nights with him! Once hung on the wall, you can use post-its to fill in the various spaces and answer questions. I leave you, below, some indications: if you need further explanations do not, I repeat NOT, contact me. You are a startupper and it is good that you learn to look for information like someone who wants to learn ... Ready-made baby food is not good for companies.

Having said that, here are a minimum of instructions to start immediately.

The Business Model Canvas is a block diagram that serves to "see" the business model you are thinking about and to identify the patterns that make it up. By pattern we mean the frequent dynamics of the business.

Each "canvas" is divided into the following nine blocks:

- Key partners: operators outside the company who collaborate in some way in the functioning of the model.
- Key resources: people, physical assets, intellectual property employed.
- Key activities: the activities carried out by the company's staff.
- Value offered: the set of peculiarities that differentiate our product / service from the competition.
- Channels: the communication and distribution channels of the good / service.
- Relations with customers: all the elements inherent to the relationship between company and customers.
- Customer segments: the various segments that make up the customer base.
- Revenue flows: the various forms of revenue that the company obtains.
- Cost structure: the structural costs that the company has to bear: variable, fixed, etc.

Lesson n. 4 (conclusion)
There are six steps to take:
Idea.
Business model. Execution.
Fundraising. Fast stairs! Exit strategies.

1   Famous forefather of role-playing games where they take on the role of a character and in which a friend acts as

narrator; it is played with paper, pen and dice.
2   A number distribution function that has the shape of a bell curve; it is named after its theorist, Carl Friedrich Gauss.
3   Online seminars; the term is given by the words seminar (seminar) and web, which become webinar.
4   Here I write it in full, in reality the correct way to indicate it is 200k, to then pronounce it "two hundred kappa"; it is the way in which, whoever handles the thousands, defines these figures; we need to know this detail, more than anything else to get used to it and not burst out laughing when the people we want to convince to finance us use it.
5   Discussion group often used in marketing to test the launch of products or ideas by monitoring the reactions of a market sample.
6   Alexander Osterwalder, Creating business models, FAG, Milan 2012.

Lesson n. 5. Liquid business

Liquid parts!
March 14 - 8.00 am, mentor's office

«Now you know the difference between a company and a startup; but this is something everyone knows. But now I will reveal to you a secret: if you really want to be successful in this world, you don't have to realize either! "

"What do you mean?"

"I'll explain it to you from what you know. As we have seen, the problem with startups is the ease with which you think: Wow, I had a brilliant idea, now only the small detail of making it is missing, and the economic empire will come by itself; let's go talk to a venture ... We understand this strategy doesn't work. "

We nodded.

"The strategy that instead allows a startupper to be credible is to make the idea work at least a little before meeting the lenders."

We nodded again.

"I see you agree with me, but what do you think it means to make it work at least a little?"

We remained silent: we did not know.
«It means making it real and concrete. And the only way to make an idea real and concrete, in the world of capitalists, is to start a company that profits from that idea! " He drew a circle on the board and broke three slices into a pie chart. "Here's the strategy to implement before meeting a venture capitalist," he said.

"So we have to create a company?" I asked.

«Take it easy: we have seen the problem you usually have with startups; but what are the problems you have with companies? "

We did not venture into the answer.

«In most cases, a company is born from a person who is good at doing something on behalf of someone else, who thinks: Why should I keep making my boss rich ?! And he sets up his own business. "

"Theoretically correct reasoning."

"Yes, but also practically wrong: because when he realizes it, that person realizes that being a pastry chef is very different from running a pastry shop, and he finds himself having to face the following problems:

- Taxes too high.

- Challenging bureaucracy.
- High personnel costs.
- Expenses not foreseen.
- Managerial inability.
- Etc.

«All problems that are resolved only having familiarity with the trade as an entrepreneur."

"So we have to ... learn to be entrepreneurs ?!"

«It would be appropriate, but no: you don't have time to learn how to do it

entrepreneurs, because you are already committed to learning the job of startupper."

"However we do not have to not even act like there most of startuppers, who only show up with the idea in their pocket, without having built the company."

"Exactly: you have to get out of this paradox!"

"How you do it?"

"You tell me."

"By putting someone with entrepreneurial experience in society?"

«That is a next step, implementing it now would be a risk: you do not have the skills to evaluate its preparation, nor subsequently its work; you would be too dependent on this person and the company would no longer be yours; no: this path is viable, but it is a subsequent step, believe me. "

"What do you propose to do then?"

"You have to create a liquid company."

"Liquid ?!"

«Liquid, yes: that is to say lean, dynamic, fast; a company that weighs as little as possible. "

"And how do you create a liquid company?"

"It used to be nearly impossible to even think of it; today, thanks to the internet, a kid can delegate practically any kind of service from his room! "

"Where do we start?"

«Start by streamlining the steps: first think about how your company should work, then start removing. Then simplify again! "

Simplify again. The guidelines were clear: without offices, at low cost, with as few staff as possible.

"This is your job! All that you can outsource, delegate it, abandon the idea of having your own place and rather take a workspace in an office; make sure you can work wherever you are thanks to a web connection, give up ties as much as you can: you must be able to move and change country at any time! "

«Change country? Why?"

"Young people like to complain that the place where they live offers few possibilities, but they don't talk about changing country, they stay where they are inventing more or less plausible excuses. Remember that if you find someone willing to finance you, they will want to keep you close and close: do you remember the 80-mile rule? "

"Well..."

"In the email I sent you it was explained that in Silicon Valley you don't invest in anything more than 80 miles from the city: if you want our money, move the company headquarters and the work team to us, they tell you."

"I guess it doesn't apply only to Silicon Valley ..."

"Indeed: you never invest too far." I smiled. "Investors don't like driving ?!"

He answered my smile. "Let's say they prefer to be in control."

"Control?"

"The ability to swoop into the office at any time: that's why they'll gladly provide you with one next to theirs, if you don't have one!" He winked at me and I did

I felt uncomfortable.
"It looks like a threat ..."
"It's the equivalent of due diligence." 1
I looked at him puzzled, I didn't know what a due diligence was; he understood my hesitation and cut it short.
«Castello them, their rules: it's not the startups that are missing, the investors are the hard thing to find; and this, whoever invests, knows it well. "
"So a company that's easy to transfer, huh ?!" I liked traveling: Ok, go for the globetrotter, I thought.
Just when it seemed done, he added, "One last thing: no relatives, friends or girlfriends; I absolutely forbid you to involve them in the project! Business is business: if people do not 'turn around', they must be immediately removed and replaced with others; and firing your girlfriend is always problematic. "
"And to hire staff, how do we do it?" I objected. "Salaries cost ..."
«The solution is: fewer employees and more suppliers; no contracts, better professionals for complex things and interns for simpler ones. Furthermore, it

could be useful to break up the realization of a project among several suppliers, so as not to give a product made, finished and ready to be launched to a known supplier. And forget about giving stock options to the first comer, even if he looks like a god on Earth. "

Nice nerve to give us such advice, it was pretty much what we had done with him! However, the vision was clear: a company designed in this way was certainly not destined to become a large company, but it could have easily guaranteed us initial income and did not involve much business risk; furthermore, the most important advantage was that it allowed us to introduce ourselves to financiers with an already functioning system!

"The rule you have to keep in mind is: think big but start light, if you want to climb quickly!" summed up.

"What you have to do," our mentor continued, "is to create a prototype."

"A prototype?"

"Exactly: do you know how the balloon was born?"

Of course we didn't know: he didn't even pause to wait for an answer.

"When the Montgolfier brothers presented the project on paper, they were ridiculed by the other scientists: the simple idea of a balloon flying in hot air was unthinkable! Then they made a miniature of it with little funds. On 19 September 1783 they flew her to the palace of Versailles, covering a distance of about 3 kilometers at almost 500 meters high, carrying a rooster, a goose and a sheep. Queen Marie Antoinette and Louis XVI saw her take off. At that point it was easy to find investors for their startup. "

"I understand why things turned out like this," I said. "The first time they failed because they only came up with the idea ... later they created their execution instead!"

«Now it's up to you: create yours! Think big, start light and scale fast: 2
is the motto of Silicon Valley! "

Lesson n. 5 (continued)

Create a "liquid" company. The scheme is: Create the company. Make it work. Go to the venture.
Nobody finances the project of a balloon, but many will finance the balloon in flight. Create a prototype!

FROM THE SHARED FOLDER IN DROPBOX

Practical tips for creating a PROTOTYPE

Dear guys, producing a prototype, in practice, can mean different things depending on the business you are creating. For example, if it is a physical business such as a local or a chain of stores, creating a prototype means creating a first pilot exercise; in this case the parameters to choose are the following:

- Identify a bomb location; do not try to do things in the average: that first example will have to convince investors to invest, so if you find unique and unrepeatable conditions, pursue them: do not worry about not being able to repeat that uniqueness in the future, opportunities happen for a reason, have faith!
- Create the procedures to make everything work without you and do nothing yourself: if things work because you work on them, you will never be able to disengage!

If, on the other hand, you are dealing with physical products, or real inventions, have the various "pieces" made separately: it is okay that having an NDA signed at the first meeting is an amateur mistake, but protecting yourself is not always wrong, and since confidentiality agreements can be circumvented or broken, choose multiple customers to make the various parts of the product separately and have them assembled by a third party. It costs a little more but protects you from nasty surprises.

Same thing goes for software development: commission the implementation of the various algorithms and codes separately.

To save on resources I recommend that you choose:

- For commissionable jobs, outsourcing through freelancers. The best choice falls on platforms such as freelancer.com through which tenders can be held to commission the work to the resource that convinced us the most.
- To create software (such as apps, websites or programs in general), the resources of third world countries are the best choice; my team of pakistani, forfor example, he works for $ 3 an hour and is happy to do so. You can direct the work

quietly from your home through web conferences.

Co-working
11.00, always in the mentor's office

We had been at work for three hours: we used the mentor's office as a base; from his desk the idea of the liquid company that would serve as a prototype was beginning to take shape. We showed the results as we went along: "We can use loaner offices for the offices."
Most of the time the mentor listened to our plans and nodded. Every so often, as in this case, he would throw us suggestions. "Remind me to tell you about co-working."
"What are co-working?"
«They are shared offices made available free of charge or at low cost for projects like yours. I'll take you to visit some of them when we have time. "
It was all so fast; we were bombarded with information and by now I felt like I was launched. I continued with my exposition: «Initially we will renounce any form of advertising, including word of

mouth; we won't even talk about it with our most trusted friends ».

"Remember why we do it: we want to introduce ourselves to the ventures ..."

"It is precisely for this reason: I would like the project to come to light only after the first concrete results, to give the impression of sudden growth."

"Quite right. Let's talk about the type of company. "

"We were thinking of a business association."

The mentor snapped: an alarm bell had sounded in his head.

"Absolutely not, no oddities: choose the corporate model you prefer, as long as it is a joint stock company!"

"Well, you don't give us a great choice: Srl or SpA ... there is nothing else!"

«The reasoning applies to any place you choose to leave: Ltd if you are in England, Sarl in Luxembourg and so on. The important thing is that you exclude everything in between: low cost alternatives such as cooperatives, simplified companies and the like only show that you are the first to disbelieve in the idea. "

"But if we have to limit costs, why throw them into the establishment of a company?"
"They are not thrown away at all: they are invested in credibility."
"Explain yourself better."
"If to save a few thousand euros you come up with an improvised corporate structure, the impression you give is that you don't want to take risks on your project first."
"Okay, but who's putting the money?" You?"
"The 10% that I deserve, of course."
"And the others? We are at zero, we put everything we had in the beta-test. "
"This was a mistake: you shouldn't have worn them if you have a few. I will answer the question 'Where do we find the money to leave?' when the problem will arise,

therefore we postpone the discussion to that moment; meanwhile, write a note: lack of money is not an obstacle. Ignorance is an obstacle. "
"Ignorance?"
"You don't know where to go to get them, right ?!" He had convinced me. I wrote everything down.

13.27, lunch break

"Come with me."
We went out. A black sedan with driver was waiting for us.
"The company treats you well, you managers!"
"It's not the company car," he replied. "It's Uber."
"Uber?"
"Yes, I usually travel by taxi: it's cheaper than owning a car; however this is an interesting case history that I wanted to tell you about, a startup in which I wish I had invested so much. As we went down the stairs you saw me calling: I was sending a request for a driver. "
The interior of the car was particularly luxurious. "Yes but ... how much exactly does it cost?"
«Little more than a taxi, but that's not the point: study their case history, it's more interesting. Indeed, take this code, if you use it when you download the application, we will both receive a credit to try the service. Can you tell me what this bonus is for? "
"To encourage word of mouth ... to increase population!"

"Precisely: we too should invent a similar mechanism for your startup."
"Where are we going now?"
"At the office."
"I do not understand. Which office? "
"Yours, if you like."
"I still do not understand."
"You will understand."
The car stopped in front of an anonymous building in a suburban neighborhood. The lobby was well kept, the doorman wore a formal uniform, which is rare in Italy, and he greeted us smiling with an Anglo-Saxon: "Can I help you?" instead of our own: "Say", and I liked this. The elevator led directly into the office, which provided a certain "wow effect"; I liked that too. As the doors opened we found ourselves in front of a loft with workstations scattered everywhere. "Stations" wasn't exactly the right word; the environment, almost totally open space, looked like an amusement park: there were spaces to sit and work in the most disparate solutions: from cushions thrown on the ground to a treadmill connected to a monitor to hold conference-calls while walking. Obviously pinball machines and table football in the relaxation corner, which did not differ

from the rest of the room in decor and style except for the presence of games, even a very dated original video game cabinet with Ms. Pac-Man directly from the Eighties; that alone, in my opinion, would have been a valid reason to work there;

nevertheless it was immediately noticed that, despite the effect of improvised spaces, everything had been studied by a skilled interior design. I paused in front of the only "closed" room, a glass cube with transparent walls, inside which a meeting seemed to take place: a boy was showing a graph to two admiring ladies.
"Nice aquarium, huh ?!" a girl who was examining a graph in Excel, sitting on the ground, legs crossed, with her laptop on her lap, told me.
"Right now a pitch for the financing of a startup is taking place," a beautiful hipster told us, hurrying to join us.
"It's not a pitch, it's a seed," my mentor pointed out. I nodded as if I knew what he was talking about, promising myself to ask him the meaning of those "supercazzole" once alone.
The girl, who had probably started a sentence automatically, stopped it in the

middle. "Good morning, you have an appointment with ... ah, it's her!" Our mentor was obviously a regular because the beautiful girl was partying him like a puppy.

"Who brought us, boss?"

"Friends; they are two startuppers with an interesting project, can you take us for a ride? "

The so-called tour was practically a sale of space; space that was somehow owned by our mentor, obviously: we were shown everything we could easily notice on our own, but the banality of objects was enhanced by a different way of calling them. Each space had its own hacker-style nickname; the sofas were «generic seats», the relaxation room and the meeting room respectively «antistress corner» and «aquarium»; I don't hide that it was funny, but judging by the concentrated faces around me, I had a strong suspicion that it would only be fun for the first week. While I was thinking, listening and mentally jotting down funny names for idiotic things, I looked at our mentor and with my eyes I sent him the only question that was buzzing in my head: Why am I here? It felt like a nerd's paradise. The tour ended fairly quickly around a meeting table that hid a pool table inside, in the room that also doubled as a rest room. The girl offered us cinnamon coffee, with cinnamon on the side, which she wanted to specify, in full Starbucks style.

"We also put an old pinball machine in the meeting room, huh ?!" She nodded.

"Now we have all the startup clichés!"

He was a little disappointed; I didn't mind that for once I wasn't the victim of my mentor's sarcasm; I wanted to know what exactly the people in that room were doing and why we were there. As if reading my head, common knowledge broke the silence induced by the sips of the soup we were drinking. "Is there anything planned?"

"Yes, it starts in half an hour."

"Well, we'll attend too: free three seats, please."

The girl jumped from the chair and took three sheets of paper, scribbled on them CONFIDENTIAL and taped them on the armchairs in the common room.

"What do you think?"

"Space is fun, but what do we need all of this?"

«This is co-working: a shared space where teams of startuppers develop their entrepreneurial projects. It works like this: you pay a small fee or get sponsored, so to speak, to stay a while. You would have the advantage of sharing the spaces with other entrepreneurs or aspiring ones like you, taking advantage of such a place, and in addition you could enjoy other benefits, for example meeting some scouts from time to time who, on behalf of ventures and investment funds , they come to find out what's interesting around. "

Now it was clear: this is what those kids around us were doing; it was obvious enough to think about it, they looked like our copy, in fact: same clothes, same attitudes, identical posture, expressions and ways of doing things. I understand why we didn't have the slightest hope of impressing at our first meeting: who knows how many had seen pass, like us! I tried to understand better.

"In here it looks like an American college fraternity: it's full of games, colorful stations, ping-pong, foosball ... it doesn't look like a workplace and it's very different from your office."

"For heaven's sake, I would never work in here! However this style has become a must from Google onwards. "

We looked at it as if the expression "from Google onward" wasn't ridiculous in itself, plus there was this arcade space serving as a common office; he went on his way without noticing.

«This place is mine, I set it up with a couple of partners and we need it as an incubator for the projects that occasionally come our way; no use for old people like me, these spaces are used to stimulate kids like you. I, too, was puzzled the first time I saw rooms like these filled with top-notch computer engineers. Perhaps I had the same expression as you when I raised these identical objections to the person who had accompanied me. I was in the lobby of the Facebook office, between a ping-pong table and a bar video game; my mentor at the time replied that those who were hired in that company usually received more or less similar proposals at the same time from the major companies in Silicon Valley, and explained to me that sometimes the choice between a contract and identical job prospects, it was given by jokes like the company that had the best sushi restaurant or the best set up play area; they even ended up asking the computer engineers which video game they preferred to have in their room.

«Computer engineers who choose the company to work in based on the best video game? At a time when every teenager has had a playstation in their room since the age of thirteen ?! " We looked at him perplexed.

"Well, it's better than throwing a coin in the air ..."

He definitely had his own way of responding to objections. Or rather: he had no interest in answering our objections.

"So you've been to Silicon Valley?"

"Yes, a lot of times: haven't you read my posts?"

"Have you been to Google's Mountain View office?"

"Yup!"

"And how?"

"The happiest place on earth! A Disneyland for programmers! Imagine an entire amusement park with all kinds of games available to its employees: swimming pools in which to swim against the current, football and beach volleyball fields, gyms, restaurants and even valets who park your car when you are late. "

"It looks like paradise!"
"It is! A friend of mine went to work there for a while. The first day they asked him what they could do to make him feel better; after a week he still hadn't found an answer: he said he couldn't think of anything that could be improved. "
"But why doesn't your office have this style? You too work with startuppers. "
"This is an industry standard: we need to attract interesting kids and speak their language. Entertainment seems to have become part of co-working. They care about the form, but not about the substance behind it... It is right that Google should be like this, but that approach is not suitable for everyone (this other companies do not understand). Google must be fun and stimulating, while the office that should choose the startuppers that I like is the one you could have found in Sparta, if the Spartans had loved companies! "

Soon a presentation began inside the office. It was led by young people who sponsored an incubator for the promotion of services dedicated to startups. I better understood the dynamics of that place: a co-working was a workspace open to professionals and workers. A place where different groups of people, who do not necessarily work in the same sector or in the same project, work by sharing the space and resources of a normal office. The business of a co-working is as much to host the spaces "for rent" as to sponsor the interventions of companies that promote themselves, and to relate the companies with the "accelerators" that can help them to realize the business. The more co-working is able to do this, the better and at a higher price it can sell its workspaces.

Returning to the office, our mentor asked us if we were interested in taking a space within that structure to develop our project; he wanted to specify that we would have it for free.

"Go for the co-working. But not one of the ones we have seen: we would like to use your office; can you have a space on your desk? "

Our mentor smiled. "Absolutely not! Are you crazy? I like to work alone! " He looked at me and I was dumbfounded for a second, then smiled again. "But if you are satisfied with the next room you can have it all, the desk!" I smiled in turn.

"I'll call the warehouse right away to have you brought one up!"

While we waited, he endorsed my choice with his considerations on the matter. "Coworking is for those who don't have the contacts to create them: you already have me, what do you need a 'hook' to share with twenty or thirty other startups like yours?"

"I agree!"

It was done: we had an official headquarters where to receive and invite people, an operational office and a space in which to work; and the best news was that it cost us nothing. Nothing... apart from the 10% we would have given our mentor in exchange for his help.

Lesson n. 5 (conclusion)

Co-working is not used to scrounge an office, but to create the right contacts. Foosball in the office is a cliché!

Choose the company name you prefer, as long as it is a capital company.

Lack of money to leave is not an obstacle. aa... and where the hell should we get them ?!

1   Investigative process put in place to assess the status of a company or business.
2   Think big, start lean, scale fast; Eric Ries, The Lean Startup, Crown Publishing Group, New York 2011.

Lesson n. 6 Business accelerator

A startupper is a problem solver
March 16 - 7.00 am, new office

"Well, let's talk about how to find the money to leave!"
I had been waiting for that lesson since I met him, indeed, it can be said that it was precisely for this reason that we had met him the first time.
"Most would-be startuppers can't even get started with the idea, and the excuse they have to justify their failure is a lack of money."
"But what would the real reason be?" I asked.
"The lack of will ..."
I had sniffed such a response from the tone of his voice and was already a little prejudiced: therefore, perhaps, I was more aggressive than I wanted. "Lack of will? Would they be little motivated? "
My mentor looked at me with the air of someone who quickly got tired of speaking to a class that doesn't listen, but he was strangely polite in answering me. "I was not finished: what I was saying is lack of will combined with lack of imagination."

I was annoyed by his staid air and decided to go after him. "Can't it just be that they don't know where to find the money?"

"I grant you. However Einstein said: 'Imagination is more important than knowledge', and, speaking of himself, he continued: 'It's not that I'm smarter than others, it's just that I think longer about a problem'. "

«Forget Einstein: you yourself have stated that the lack of money is not the problem and that the problem is the lack of knowledge. You're contradicting yourself, aren't you? "

"You see, there are actually two types of problems one has to deal with when building a start-up: the real problems and the fake ones. The real problems are real and have the power to slow us down; fake problems are imaginary and have the power to stop us, because we consider them insurmountable and we give up acting. Whenever the answer to a problem is: 'I don't know' or: 'We can't', we are faced with a fake problem that blocks us. "

"This is just motivational chatter. Can you give us a concrete example? "

«It's easy to do: let's say that for our startup we need to open in China;

unfortunately, however, we have the obstacle of the language. The fake problems that could block us are: Chinese is a difficult language, or we are not inclined to learn languages. These so-called problems are not objective facts, they are opinions, and they depend on our way of seeing reality, on what we believe. On the contrary, an objective fact is that Chinese is not our mother tongue and that it will take time to learn to speak it. "

"I understand: the time and effort required to learn Chinese is the real problem that slows us down."
"Exactly. Now, what I am saying is that finding money is not a real problem that slows us down if one is willing to go through the trouble of finding that money. As for knowledge, this is a false problem! Anyone who complains of not knowing
finding financing, drawing up a business plan or looking for a crowdfunder, 1 has never really looked for the answers. And the same goes for those who do not know these terms: they never asked the questions, wrongly, otherwise they would have corrected him by teaching him the appropriate terms. These people are able

to bother a search engine to find out the times of the films in the cinema, to enter a cinema forum to discuss the plot, but they do not bother in the same way to know the date of the next startup weekend or which seminar. attend or download a business model to find out how to write an effective presentation. Believe me: lack of knowledge is a false problem. "
I wrote the key passages of that reasoning:

Lack of knowledge is a false problem.
Lack of money is a false problem.
Real problems slow us down. False problems stop us.

My mentor was clear in affirming these truths of his: he had an almost dictatorial aura and, to be honest, I understood the reasons: the absolutism with which bar chatter often crushes aspiring startuppers I knew all too well and that simple and clear way of looking at things was a clear contrast.
«Ok, I don't want to be like one of those who get blocked by the false problem: tell us everything! Now I'll ask you an open and comprehensive question: let's start from scratch and tell us, as if we didn't

know anything, where to find the money to leave, who to ask, what questions to ask and how to ask them! "

The mentor looked at us in silence: he seemed to be preparing for a sports competition... a marathon or a long swim. Finally he broke the delay. "Well, make yourself comfortable: this will take some time!"

Lesson n. 6 (continued)

If a problem has the power to block you, it means it's a false problem; real problems can at best slow you down.
The words of numbers
7.59 am, breakfast at the self service machine, corridor

"Have you ever seen A Fistful of Dollars?"
"No, is it a western?"
"It's actually a spaghetti western, do you know the difference?"
«Well, spaghetti westerns are made by Italian directors. What else is there to know? "
«Spaghetti westerns are Italian reinterpretations of American westerns; we could call them a false improvement. 2 Like those counterfeit watches which,

precisely because they are counterfeit, work better than the originals; for example, they keep the time more
precise or better resistant to water than the brand model: it doesn't happen often, but
when it happens we can say that we are faced with a false improvement. Here, spaghetti westerns are the false enhancement of the American western; real Arizona is less Arizona than the Sicilian or Spanish countryside in which Sergio Leone's films were shot. For a fistful of dollars it is precisely the progenitor of that genre, and its most representative film. Now: in that movie there is a scene where the villain, hitting the target several times with a sniper rifle, says to the hero:

When a man with a gun meets a man with a gun, the man with a gun is a dead man.

"A catchphrase."
"For you it's the same thing: only instead of guns and rifles there are words and numbers! In fact, whether it is a bank, an institution, a private association or even a friend, when you ask someone for money

for your project there is a rule that is more or less similar:

When a man with words meets a man with numbers, the man with words is a dead man.

"What does it mean?"
"It means that if you show up armed only with words, you're dead at this game!"
"But ... in the film at the end the man with the gun prevails over the one with the rifle ?!"
«Yes, but only because he prepared well and because he was very lucky: you must be prepared, have the right tools, try and try again and finally, but only ultimately, also rely on a little luck. "
I wrote everything down in my notebook:

Luck
=
1. Be prepared.
2. Having the right tools.
3. Repeat the attempt a sufficient number of times.

"Okay," I said, "how do you get lucky?"
"Let's start by speaking the right language!" He passed us his notes. "There

are some words in this world that you must necessarily know in order to speak the language

of lenders. This is the so-called language of numbers. This is a minimal vocabulary. " So saying, the mentor handed us a list he had prepared for us. He explained his point of view to us, I listened to everything carefully and wrote it down in my notes; here is the result.

The language of numbers
Your ideas are of no interest to whoever has to give you money; if what you are carrying are only words, it is useless. At most you can burn the public funding of some European tender, but you will not combine anything else.
If, on the other hand, you enter the game as protagonists, money is not a problem, but you must be able to speak the language of numbers.
Here are eleven phrases you need to learn to use when you tell me about your project:

1. Business plan: the business plan. It is a document that describes the project, complete with numbers and

forecast of costs and earnings. In the case of startups, it also has an additional document called the executive summary (which we will discuss later) which summarizes the key points.

2. Way out: the exit strategy. Each investment must include at least one, preferably two (a plan B if the first fails). It is the way in which investors are expected to return from the investment, aside from corporate profits. A typical way out for startups is listing on the stock exchange.

3. Budget: this is a forecast or estimate of costs and revenues related to the project; is the first reference in terms of figures and numbers.

4. Provisional income statement: it is the detailed forecast by expense items of how much will be spent and earned to implement the business; it is usually drawn up monthly or quarterly.

5. Cash plan: these are cash movements; while the budget and income statement relate to theoretical movements such as invoices or expected expenses, the cash register relates to real money passing through the accounts. To understand the difference: an invoice issued or received that is not paid is a

theoretical movement that concerns the income statement but for which there is no real cash movement: in theory that money is paid or collected, in practice not.

6. ROI (return on investment): indicates the ability of the business project to remunerate the invested capital. It is calculated by dividing the incomeoperating (gross profit) for the invested capital.

7. ROE (return on equity): measures the profitability of the equity invested in the business. It is calculated by dividing the net profit by the equity.

8. EBITDA (gross operating margin): is a profitability indicator that highlights the income of a company based only on its characteristic management, gross, therefore, of interest (financial management), taxes (fiscal management), depreciation of assets and depreciation . GOM is more important than profit for investors because it allows you to clearly see if the company is able to generate wealth through management

operational. It is what "remains" of the revenues after having borne direct costs (ie those strictly inherent to production).

9. EBIT: acronym for earnings before interests and taxes. In Italian it is defined as a "pre" result of financial expenses or as company operating income, which are two ways to indicate the same thing: how are we doing before paying taxes? It's importantfor our investors (and for us) above all because it indicates how much the company makes (how much it has returned) before remunerating the capital, i.e. paying both debt (third party capital) and equity (equity) . It is used to calculate the ROI through the formula ROI = EBIT / net invested capital.

10. EBITA: acronym of earnings before interests, taxes and amortization; means profit before interest, taxes and amortization of intangible assets. It is important because it indicates the net operating margin of a company (a synonym of the Italian MON). In practice, it is the income generated by the asset net of amortization and depreciation (ie tangible fixed assets) but not intangible fixed assets. In practice, it is the EBITDA, once the provisions and depreciation have been subtracted, that is to say the operating income.

11. EBITDA: acronym of earnings before interests, taxes, depreciation and amortization; means profit before interest expense, taxes and depreciation on tangible and intangible assets. It is important to know EBITA and EBIT and their differencesespecially in relation to EBITDA. The EBITDA of your company is the financial index that investors will look at when they evaluate whether it is worthwhile or not to invest in your project: because it shows the economic situation of the company before the entrepreneur has time to "play" with numbers; let me explain: since it photographs "how you are made money" before you insert amortization, taxes and depreciation (which can often represent fictitious costs inserted ad hoc), EBITDA is the most reliable financial index (because is the least "modifiable") to judge how interesting a company is for its ability to produce profits and generate profit. EBITDA is in fact very similar to the value of the cash flows produced by a company, and therefore provides the most significant indication in order to evaluate its value. It can also be used to calculate the operating result of a company, starting from the gross profit,

subtracting the taxes, depreciation, depreciation and interests of the company itself. If the costs are greater than the revenues, there will be a loss, while if the revenues are greater than the costs, you will have a profit.

"And this, as far as your company is concerned; now let's try to understand what terms you will be dealing with trying to move in this world. Let's start from the beginning: what am I to you? "
"Easy. Our mentor! "
«Exactly, but not only this: mentor is a term that you can use outside the context of startups; actually in recent years there has been a boom in professional figures linked to the coaching market and, sometimes, mentorng mixes with these figures. You have to tell me what I am from your startup's point of view. "
We didn't know how to answer.

"Of course you don't know; let's see if you can figure it out for yourself without me explaining it to you. I have prepared a little game for you ... it's like for The Puzzle Week: on the one hand you will find the terms, on the other the definitions; associate each term with the correct definition."

TO   Hedge fund   1
B.   Private   2
equity

The one who supports mutual funds and management companies, offering investors industrial experience, strategic business vision, quality leadership, expert evaluation of business opportunities and qualitative and temporal analysis of investment proposals.

Risk capital provided by professional investors to support newly formed companies, in the initial stages of their development, with high income potential but also high financial needs.

Any fund that uses a strategy or set of strategies other than simple

C.   Company advisor

3   purchase of bonds, shares (mutual funds) and credit securities (money market funds), whose purpose is the achievement of an absolute return.

D. Business advisor

4   financial activity through which an investor acquires company shares in a company by acquiring the shares, and invests capital within the same.

Otherwise, said informal investor, is a manager, an entrepreneur and more generally a professional, still in business or retired, with a substantial

Venture capital 5

F. Crowdfunding   6

G. Business angel   7

personal assets, a good network of contacts, a fair propensity to risk, willing to invest in small-medium enterprises, through participation in risk capital, in the startup and other early financing phases, with the aim of obtaining a high return on investment.

The director and / or consultant able to support and support a company in the delicate phases of startups, mergers and acquisitions, and sale of the business or parts of it.

Economic financing process provided, individually, by a large number of individuals from all over the world to finance a project with a sum set in advance.

"But ... how do we do it if we don't know ..."
"Get there by logic: I'll give you a little help: start with what I'm doing for you!"
I looked through the list more carefully. "Ok, what are you to us?"
"It seems obvious to me: a business angel!" I associated name and definition: one was done! G5.
We continued the exercise. We identified all the correct combinations (A3 - B4 - C1 - D6 - E2 - F7 - G5), and understood that, more than us, our mentor needed to understand how familiar we were with some terms and how much we used them without really knowing them the meaning. He added that the superficial preparation is noticeable, and that using terms at random only for emulation makes aspiring startuppers branded as wannabes, putting them in a bad light in front of the possible financier. He told us of a time when he proposed a joint venture between a large credit institution and a small company of his; he described

the response he received as "not exactly encouraging" and in the evening I found this untitled document in a subfolder of Dropbox.

FROM THE SHARED FOLDER IN DROPBOX
Untitled document
Dear guys, here is the answer I received for misusing the term
"Joint venture" when I presented a proposal to a bank ... If you think I'm too "hard" on you, know that it is to save you a wash of the head like this.
«I think the term 'JV' is nothing short of 'optimistic' given the insignificant size of your company and the mammoth size of the counterparty you intend to call into question. Unless you're a McKinsey, who might (and I stress could) see value in you that justifies co-branding, it's pretty hard to get something where you jointly on anything with them. Get it out of your head. And that doesn't just apply in this case - get it out of your head with any company of this type! Incidentally, not only do you make a bad impression, but also me who introduce you and, I assure you, it would bother me a little. Having said that, I will give you a brief summary

of the scenario in which you are forcibly slipping: you want to approach a company that on Friday announced the new industrial reorganization from the dead, injured and no prisoners' and whose minimum time (provided that they have budget and that my contacts in the meantime have not already been fired, moved and / or gagged and made to disappear in the concrete) of project development, from initial proposal to delivery, is 24-36 months (I tell you from personal experience). "And now, as you take them out of my hands, a couple of suggestions for dealing with me.

«If you think you will get anxious or create anxiety for me, with a pushy approach as a real estate agent for the whole 36 months of gestation, I will stop you already here and let it be; I want to be clear given the three phone calls you made to me over the weekend: personally I have NEVER received sms / emails / phone calls from an 'unknown' to fan a project that is absolutely secondary to me, written with my feet, on a client so complex ... and all while I am doing three corporate deliveries (I am writing to you while I am in a meeting with a client) when the activities related to your sector are not even an activity that I deal with.

«Either you calm down seriously and take a handful of anxiolytics or here you are not going anywhere and I immediately see any continuation of this project because I have no time to waste on projects of this type, managed in such an amateur way; nor do I intend to be stalked for this bullshit. Not even my contacts with whom I am under contract dream of sending me text messages, emails, calls to ask me 'how we are' on well-paid and well-defined strategic projects: imagine if on a project developed for free, without any certainty of closing anything is marginal with respect to my activities, I can tolerate dynamics of this type. Last warning, then stop the music and get off the carousel.

"Better safe than sorry.

THX M. "

«Here, now you know much more than before, and it is still not enough; but now you can sit down at the players table and start serving the cards. Now let's try to

understand who we should meet, when and above all why. It's like a football match: it's about choosing the players; You can't form a team if you ignore the rules, you don't know that you need a goalkeeper, two to four defenders, wings, midfielders, an attacking trident or a striker. "

"Yes, the metaphor is clear to me."

"Well, then let's try to figure out which part of the field each player covers!"

Lesson n. 6 (continued)

When a man with words meets a man with numbers, the man with words is a dead man!

If you explain the plan in words, you will receive words in exchange; if you explain the plan by numbers, you will receive numbers in response.

Training circles
10.00 am, office

"I ask you to stand up and stand in the center of the room." We ran without asking questions.

"This room represents the market. We are part of it and you are at the center of everything: you, the startuppers, with your startup idea. What you have to do is expand: fill the room, which is the market, with your project. You have to touch two opposite walls at the same time: can you do it? "

Evidently we wouldn't have been able to, so we just shook our heads.

"Let's see if it's true: try to spread your arms and touch the walls."

We performed, even though it was clearly impossible; the room was large: not even a very tall man could have made it.

"As expected, you are not capable, alone. Your company, but you knew this from the beginning, cannot expand by relying only on your means: you have to keep this in mind. "

We nodded.

"I know it sounds trivial, but the means you have at your disposal to expand the company are cumbersome, slow and sometimes very difficult to use. You will often be tempted to fall prey to optimism and think you can do everything yourself; when it happens, go back to the center of the room and try to touch two opposite walls with your fingertips and when you feel ridiculous enough, go back to looking for the means. Everything is clear?"

We nodded again.

«Well, let's see what these means are. To design the ecosystem around the startup market, a thousand different schemes can be used; I was inspired by that of Booz & Company, which takes into consideration people, companies or institutions

that contribute to the success of a business project, defining them as 'entrepreneur enablers' and representing them in a diagram made up of four concentric circles. That's how I interpret it. " He took some A4 sheets and began to write names and acronyms. He arranged the first three sheets on the ground, forming a circle around us:

"Well, the first resources you have to rely on correspond to the first 'training circle'. And there are three elements, "he said.

FIRST CIRCLE: PERSONAL ENABLERS
"The first circle concerns what we could define as 'personal culture'. This circle allows entrepreneurs to acquire the knowledge necessary to create, manage and administer a business. They provide the cultural bases to be able to move within the market and are:

- Mentors and consultants.
- Personal training.
- School education.

«The first circle is the first gap to fill: you can do it yourself. As far as school is concerned, two tasks will need to be carried out: the basic education you have will be fine, as long as you can detoxify yourself of 'middle-class' cultural references that want you to be employees on a fixed salary intent on avoiding mistakes rather than chasing success: we have already mentioned this and I do not intend to go back to it, you know what I am talking about and, if you need to refresh your memory, pick up the list of your classmates and how they ended up. The secondary and specialist education you have chosen, if you have decided to continue your studies, keep it as a reference cultural background. As for personal education, those courses that no one forces you to take e

those books that no one forces you to read, well, devour as much of those books as possible, without becoming fanatics of any particular current: the economist-pessimists and the gurus of positive thinking are both useful and harmful, if taken in excess; as with antidotes, overdose is more lethal than the poison they cure. "

"Well, a lot of the training and books you talk about are expensive ..."

"Then get them for Christmas!" Personally I have a rule for training expenses which is as follows:

Invest in training at least three times as much as you spend on travel, toys and luxury goods.

«I have always followed it and it is an investment that has paid off, in most cases, with interest! Let's move on to the second circle. "

He took four more sheets and arranged them to form a circle outside the first one:

SECOND CIRCLE: FINANCIAL ENABLERS
"Outside the first circle, which is the base, is money. This circle takes into consideration any way in which money can arrive: we can put it ourselves, with our personal finance, ask someone for it, that is to say investments with risk capital, ask banks for it or win tenders and competitions:

- Finance and micro-SMEs.
- Risk Investors.
- Banks.
- Institutional programs.

"Basically the rule is: find the money, no matter where," I ventured.
"I wouldn't say: it really matters! If it takes a little or a long time, things change a lot. The first distinction to be made is whether we are looking for debt or partners. " He wrote:

FIRST QUESTION:
Do you want to find debt or partners?

"A debt?"
"Of course! If you are looking for debt, then you can turn to the banks, or alternatively to the financial ones; you could even resort to a mortgage between individuals: the loan between individuals is active and legal also in Italy and even supported by organizations or associations, in recent years. If you don't need a lot of money and you plan to monetize quickly and you think you have very good hopes of repaying everything immediately, then you are looking for a debt! When you buy a debt, you receive

money which you will have to pay back, little by little, with interest. It is a good way to finance you, the most convenient, if the company goes well, but also the most risky! "

"On the other hand, what advantages and what risks does the alternative present?"

"It is certainly the least risky, because in this case whoever lends you the money takes part in the risks and accepts the possibility of not getting it back. However, it's also the most expensive if the business gets going. Having a partner who shares your idea at 50% can be much more expensive than paying off a mortgage! "

"What do you recommend?"

"In your case, I would say that shareholder capital is the best option: you don't have many guarantees of success, and what the partners will provide will be exclusively venture capital; it is so called because whoever supplies it accepts the risk of losing every cent. "

"I agree!"

"I'm delighted, but we're not done yet: there's a third circle." He added the third circle formed by three more sheets.

THIRD CIRCLE: COMPANY ENABLERS

"In addition to financial help, you need help from a logistical point of view. This type of support will be given to you by other companies, associations and service companies. We can divide the company enablers between:
- Professional services.
- Trade associations.
- Incubators.

"Incubators?" I had heard that term before, but I still didn't understand exactly what it meant. My mentor sensed this and gave me an overview.

"It is normal for you to be confused, because it is quite difficult to define what an incubator is. You see, technically there are companies or associations or programs that can be defined as incubators. "

"In fact, the problem is this: I often hear incubators defined as different things."

«The real problem is that you don't ask questions: you are approximate! When someone uses a term, stop and ask yourself if you understand what they are talking about: the approximation of terms kills agreements, in business! "

I deserved that pulling of the ears: I nodded without arguing. "What is an incubator?"

"I'll gladly answer you: when it comes to companies, a business incubator is a program designed with the aim of accelerating business development."

"How?"

"By providing economic, logistical and service resources to support the companies it supports."

"But who decides which and how many resources to provide, and how to offer support?"

"First of all, you must be accepted by the incubator, that is, do no more and no less than what we will see shortly, to face the various presentation rounds and pitches with venture capitalist companies."

"And who should we introduce ourselves to?" I mean: how do you knock on the door of an incubator? "

"Once the incubator chooses to support your company, you will be assigned an incubator manager who offers those services both through institutional communications and through his private network of contacts: you have to network, in essence, and know the right people , that is, among others, also incubator managers. "

"And where do they meet?"

"Well, the simplest way is through a network of relationships: the people you know, the people you don't know, but of whom you have to learn to frequent the environments to meet them 'casually', the people your people know, to whom you present and, of course, the events, fairs and seminars that the people you want to meet attend: for example, the startup weekends. "

"Damn ... it looks like a full-time job!"

«Establishing a good network of relationships is the task of every good startupper; and yes, it's a job. "

"But how do you find the time to do everything?"

"Working as a team: associating people who know how to build relationships or already have them in place."

"Comets?"

Our mentor smiled. "Well, if you have any other questions about what pitches, rounds or startup weekends are, keep them to yourself: we'll see them when we talk about that topic."

I looked at the papers scattered around me, full of acronyms and names to remember. "Things are getting complicated, huh?"

"This is why we are proceeding in concentric circles: analyze one circle at a time and everything will appear clear to you."

I made an effort to do so and, in fact, the concentric perspective greatly simplified my vision of things. "Well, maybe complicated isn't the right word, but certainly at this level things are starting to get really interesting!"

"Wait to make you dizzy: we're just in the third circle!"

"How many others are missing?"

"The last one, there are four in all."

"Thank god. I thought worse!"

"The problem with the fourth circle is that it is the most complex, and it varies from country to country like no other: it concerns the regulatory environment and who makes the laws."

"Ouch."

"Exactly." That said, the mentor placed the last circle of papers around us.

FOURTH CIRCLE: ENVIRONMENTAL ENVIRONMENTS

- Legal context.
- Infrastructure.
- Media and culture.
- Lobby and business organizations.

«There aren't many explanations to give on this last circle: the media, the power lobbies, the bureaucracy and obviously the laws influence the outcome of your business; Needless to say, the more you have these infrastructures on your side, the more chance you have of bringing home a

prosperous and profitable business. "
"I understand."
"Now look around you and analyze the way forward: remember that your aim is to fill the room, that is, to saturate the market as much as possible with your products and / or services."
The point was clear: so far we had moved haphazardly, from one circle to another, without logic. We were looking for formal investors before clarifying to ourselves if we wanted a debt or a shareholder, and we attempted a dialogue with institutions or entities without a clear distinction and without knowing exactly what to ask for.

The risk, as we had experienced all too well, was that of getting burned, wasting time and not doing anything! We looked at the concentric circles around us trying to figure out how to fill them all. Our mentor sensed the discouragement and explained: "I'm not saying you need everything, just that you need most of these tools: the more you have, the more chance you will have to make it."

Forcing myself to understand, I asked: "Okay, what if instead they finance us right away and we start working without having these tools?"

He pointed to two opposite walls of the room, and said, "Could you touch them, please?" I understood the message, so I nodded, but he stopped me. "I'm asking you to do it:

first touches one wall, then the other. " I ran even though I felt ridiculous.

«So, theoretically, if you are fast enough, you can be able to touch both walls at the same time: you just need to exceed the speed of light. Now, since this is impossible in practice, to avoid going back and forth like a top, you should master as many tools as possible. The more you go outwards, the more these tools become accessories, but they are still important. "

"And yet, I understand that there are also companies that don't own them all, don't they?"

"Of course, but it's a risk: you won't have them all either, but you should master as many as possible: do you remember the car rental company with which we reached co-working?"

"Of course: Uber."

"You may not know it, but following the success of their service, they have decided to launch a low cost version that allows individual citizens in possession of a car to improvise as taxi drivers: they have launched it in various countries ..."

«But ... can they do it ?! Don't you need a license or what do I know ?! "

"This is exactly the point: the regulations of the fourth circle are not the same in every country; here, for example, there are problems: you can't decide out of the blue to be a taxi driver, you need a license! "

"I understand what you mean: if our startup has an international scope ..."

"... and we long for it to be so!" added the mentor.

"... then the problems related to the fourth circle have multiplied ..."
"Exactly, stay lean: the bureaucracy thrives on complicated things! And get ready to fight anyway! "
"Fight?" I asked.
"Look," he said, handing us a statement.
He gave us a folder full of scattered papers: newspaper excerpts, photocopies of controversies

from blogs and magazines, links to websites: some reported the polemics with the public administration, other statements by ministers, still others protest marches; the sheer amount of news made me nauseous just looking at her.
«I keep this envelope as a warning for young startuppers like you: I can ask the secretary to send you a copy, if you think it is appropriate; it is used like this: browse it when you are tempted to underestimate the regulatory aspects related to your innovative businesses. "
He smiled, but the message was clear.
"There is no need, we understand!"
"Better this way." He put the heavy binder back on the top shelf, then picked up the papers from the floor and placed them

neatly in a folder. "Well, we're done with the circles: that's all, are there any questions?"

Lesson n. 6 (conclusion)

The more tools you have, the more solid you are.
It is extremely rare to have all the tools.
The bigger you get, the more important the fourth circle becomes!

1   An entity that allows financing by multiple investors entering small stakes; we'll talk about it later.
2   If you want to know more, I invite you to read the Django Unchained review by Casanova Wang Kar-Way on the website www.i400calci.com. Even if you are not curious, go there anyway: they are brilliant.

Lesson n. 7. Fundraising

Find the money to leave
March 16 - 11.00, coffee break

"To tell the truth, I still have the initial question: how do we find the money to leave?"
«But ... are you serious? I just explained it to you! "
"Not at all: you explained the theory, tell us what we have to do in practice."
"I don't understand, what else do you want to know ?!"
«Don't be pretend to be stupid: the circles you've created around us... it's all very clear, really, enlightening! But they are only tools that we need to move better once we leave: they do not answer the original question, the one we started with, and that is: Where do I find the money to leave? "
"Agree. What do you want me to specifically explain? "
He had remarked on the last word; I noticed it because it was a technique used in neurolinguistic programming that I had studied some time ago; I was starting to warm up, but I kept my cool. «What I would like you to explain to me are the

concrete actions to be carried out in order to collect the amount we need to leave; the pattern you have drawn at our feet is good for understanding the world of startups, but I want to understand how to get money into our coffers! A series of actions to be carried out specifically: step number one, number two, number three ». I remarked the word the same way, hoping he would notice.

"So you would like a procedure, am I right?"

"Call it what you like: I want instructions to follow, something that works!"

The mentor smiled pleased and satisfied. The smile was followed by a deep breath, and the breath by a blatant applause. "Good boy. You have not given up: so do you. Where to find the money to leave, huh ?! Now I'll explain it to you. "

I was perplexed: was it really a test or did he play it very well? I never would have known; but the important thing was to get answers.

«Most startuppers do not know how to distinguish the various levels of fundraising; they think the search for capital consists in the simple act of asking for money to finance the idea. They completely ignore what is called the funding circle, namely the treasure map that explains where to dig to unearth the chest depending on what stage you are in. I will give you that map, but only if you accept the fact that, currently, you do not have it: when you came to the meeting with an idea and asked for a loan, you moved randomly, and did not have the slightest chance of receiving money. Do you understand now? "

"Yes, I understood it immediately, looking at the circles."

"Well. So first I must teach you to distinguish what type of financing you are asking for and why; once this is done we will identify together with whom to make that request; finally I will explain how, giving you all the necessary tools. "

"Do you mind if you sign it to me?" I wouldn't want you to digress further: this time I want to get to the point! "

"Go ahead." I ran:

Step n. 1: distinguish the type of financing we are looking for. Step n. 2: identify who to make the request.

Step n. 3: understand how to do it: receive the tools to do it.

«However, I would like to point out that mine are not digressions at all. If I don't prepare you to receive the information, that information is useless, like seeds thrown into unplowed land: they take root with difficulty. "

I nodded with little conviction.

«We assume that what we are talking about is not called 'Financing a startup': this expression is inappropriate. What you are talking about when you say: 'Get the money to leave' is called seeding. "

"What does it mean?"

«A seed is a seed. Seeding means 'sowing'. You are grappling with seeding, and this means that you don't have a thriving company yet, but you have a plant or maybe not even that: pot and soil. "

A seed, I repeated to myself.

"In Italy we don't know much about this difference: in fact, 99% of the loans that are passed off as fundraising are actually seeding."

"I understand, but what difference does it make what they are called?"

"You don't understand at all. Much of the statistics that tell how thriving and growing the startup landscape is about fundraising when most of the funding is in a range between 25 and 50k. And in many cases not even those micro-credits are able to pay for themselves with the investment! If you behave like the majority of startups and pursue this alms, you will not achieve anything: for less than 200k there are much less complicated and cheaper ways than selling your soul to a venture capitalist! "

"Are these the options you are going to teach us?"

"Exact! Listen to me carefully: even before the actual seeding, there is a passage that is not even considered in the original culture of startups, namely Silicon Valley: the one in which the initial capital is raised from scratch. "

"Isn't it considered? Why? It would seem to me the most important step! "

«I can confirm that it is: for that very reason it is taken for granted! It's a litmus test, the watershed! Think about it: how easy is it to get an idea? Anyone can do it! What blocks most people is really getting involved, finding the money to leave ... putting your face on it or risking your wallet yourself! "

"That's exactly what we're asking you to tell us!"

«I understand it. But in the culture of startups, which is the culture of those who finance them, that is venture capitalists, if you need to ask me for help because you can't even find the first 100,000 euros you need to start, you are not the horse on the which

bet."
"Are you saying that ..."
«I'm saying that a startupper is first of all a problem solver. Think about it: to find the right idea what do you do, after all? You discover a widespread problem and invent a way that does not yet exist to solve it. You use your inventiveness and your creativity; to these you add perseverance and communication skills to explain the problem and the idea. "
"Yes, that's clear to me."
"Well. And how should finding money be different? Isn't it a question also in this case of solving a widespread problem? Only in this case, the problem is yours, it affects you closely and is called lack of liquidity. "
"Yes but..."
"But you have been taught that it is a different problem that cannot be solved creatively; instead it is not at all the way things are! Saying you don't know where to find the money is like saying you don't

know where to find the winning idea: it just means you've stopped asking yourself questions! If you can't solve the widespread problems, you are not a startupper: the lack of initial capital is the most widespread of the problems! "

"So you're telling me there's no basic method?"

"No, I'm telling you there are an infinity of them! Now I'll explain what I use and what I make my startuppers use. And I will no longer talk to you about theories, but about practice. But you have to understand that you don't need my magic formula at all, you just need to scale the money into a problem to be solved and understand that you can get to grips with it thanks to the exact same resources that have allowed you to conceive the brilliant idea you intend to implement. "

It seemed to make sense.

"The methods I use are three." He opened a desk drawer and took out three envelopes: envelope number 1, envelope number 2, envelope number 3.

"What the hell is this ?!"

The mentor was amazed at my reaction. "Well ... I thought I'd explain it to you as if it were a game of prizes, after all it's not very different, do you think?"

"But you ... are you really an entrepreneur by trade ?!" We were having a show walker explain how to start the business.

"Listen, if you think serial entrepreneurs like me are boring dudes watching numbers on a screen and spending time holding meetings behind a desk, that's your problem: I have a partner who has developed a board game to teach. how to achieve financial freedom, so consider yourself lucky if I haven't put two dice in your hand and a token on the board yet! " Then he turned to both of them. "Come on, pick an envelope," he said, pointing to the three options.

My patience was reaching its limit. "Envelope number one," I sighed without much conviction.

He opened the envelope.

"Acc ... the worst option!"

"And it seemed to you!" I wasn't lucky even by pretending. "What have we won?"

"Nothing for now," he showed the contents of the envelope, a sheet of paper that read:

Public calls

"Here is the first answer: funding and contributions, state or private. Calls are periodically launched by private associations, including business incubators, of which we have spoken previously, state or regional bodies; even in times of crisis, funds are set up to finance startups or innovative projects or projects for the enhancement of the territory or local development... a bit of everything in short. If you choose this route, your task is to find the announcement, find out about how to participate and participate! "

"And is it easy to win one?"

«It depends on the announcement and the conditions; in general no... there are many who want a piece of the pie. Then of course it depends on the conditions of the call: if it is a non-repayable loan it is more difficult, because they give money and everyone wants to win this type of offer. A middle ground are low-interest mortgages, in which you have to repay, diluted over the years in installments, almost only the initial liquidity. Finally, there are the reimbursements that do not solve the liquidity problem, because the amount must be paid in advance by you first and only after some time is it reimbursed by the organization promoting the call, and following careful certifications. "

It seemed complicated. "What do we need to increase our chances of getting money through this route?" I asked.

"The short answer is: saints in heaven. And, since you're going to ask me, no, I don't have them. Because I have learned not to rely on politics and the state: too complicated, too many bureaucratic gears and too much delays. We are entrepreneurs and we need speed: endless expectations kill us! However, if you choose this path, the official answer I give you is that you need a resource that can sort out, full time or almost, any kind of call available at this moment or that will be activated shortly here. This resource cannot be improvised: it must know what to look for and find the right conditions for how to participate. Sending an application that does not meet all the selection criteria will take you out of the game immediately. Certainly a resource of this type is precious for a startup. "

"Can we pay it once the result is obtained, perhaps with a percentage of the loan received?"

"You can try to propose it to him, but I doubt that a truly qualified person, with this type of professionalism, will agree to work solely on a commission basis: the risk of getting the deck for a handful of flies is quite high!"

"Got it, and what's inside envelope number two?"

He opened the second envelope and showed us the sheet with the inscription:

Crowdfunding

«Eh, eh, eh... you will like this one; you'll lose a lot of time. " He laughed and laughed really under his mustache: it was not a pose.

"Crowdfunding, I've heard about it before, apart from the previous game: what exactly is it?"

"The principle is simple: instead of being financed a lot by a few, it is a question of being financed by so many."

"Um ... as logic would not make a turn."

"And he doesn't do it: in an old Italian film, a penniless young man, in order to conquer a princess, had to raise a considerable sum; then he makes a public appeal asking each fellow citizen for a penny ... and puts together the figure. "

"Please tell me you're not going to rely on the plot of an Italian comedy to give us the foundation for corporate financing!"

«Ah, why... did you see him ?! It is the film in which Adriano Celentano conquers Ornella Muti. But how, you ignore A Fistful of Dollars and watch these little movies? Let's go back to crowdfunding which is better! "

He always turned it around as it pleased him ... like a street vendor. I hated it when he did that, because he made me look like a market buyer too, as I was in line to buy his merchandise.

"This trend of being financed by the crowd is a phenomenon that is growing all over the world, due to the generalized restriction of bank credit. And consider that it is a recent phenomenon: the word crowdfunding was only invented in 2006 by Michael Sullivan. "

"How does it work?"

"Each crowdfunding platform makes its own story and has its own methods, but more or less they all interact through a website: the startup registers on the site and publishes what it wants to do, that is the idea, how, that is, the business plan, and with whom, the team. Then, depending on the case and the possibility, it adds the documentation to certify its value: a video, descriptive texts, financial analyzes, the opinions of other supporters, contractual pre-agreements or declarations of intent, if any. In short, all the documents useful to convince potential investors that this is a good idea.

"Who are the investors?"

«All those who register on the site; here too each platform has its parameters: in some, to register, you must commit to investing a minimum amount in at least one project within a certain period of time. "

"Okay, we don't care."

"You are interested instead, because the more reliable the investors, the more convenient it is to use that crowdfunding platform."

"So we could also end up with thousands of one-euro investors?"

"Well, most of the platforms are limited to five, six investors who cover 20% of the budget, but there are also platforms with no numerical limitations."

"If we choose crowdfunding, where would you advise us to start?"

«I'll leave you detailed notes on the steps to take in our shared folder in Dropbox; now let's open envelope number three ... "
He was eager to show us the writing:

Bootstrapping

"Wow, my favorite!"
"This is the first time I've heard from you: what's it about?"
"It's the opposite of fundraising!"
"Explain yourself better."
"Well, not quite literally, bootstrapping means getting by yourself, that is

to get out of a problem with one's own means. And it more or less means that you don't have to rely on either banks or entities, platforms or incubators. Imagine that all these things do not exist: how would you make your startup? "
I banged my fist on the table, indignant. "Are you dumb?! That's the question we've been revolving around since yesterday! "
He looked up at me, remaining impassive and calm. "I know, but I couldn't answer you right away, we first had to create the entrepreneurial background to understand the dynamics implicit in my

answer: plow the field before sowing the seeds, remember?"
He was smiling and I wanted to hit him, but I cut it short. "Ok, now we have the basics: the answer is out."
"The three fs!" she exclaimed emphatically, opening her hands in front of her face like a curtain.
"Eh ?!"

I will spare you the real dialogue that took place shortly thereafter with me insulting him and him babbling about plants and gardens to cultivate; I'll summarize the concept: you don't go to a venture capitalist asking for 100k, you go to ask for at least a million. Fundraising is not a single activity to be done only once, in which an initial amount is collected and then left: it is a constant need of the startup, which accompanies it along the various phases of the
its growth: from the foundation in the garage of house 1 to capitalization on international markets and / or to the exit. This series of steps is summarized in a more or less official scheme that is called by startuppers and investors the funding circle, but which our mentor, who was a startupper and an investor, but also an

idiot, called the treasure map. The scheme is this:

The funding circle was therefore the graphic representation of the various levels of funding. Depending on the amount of the amount (and the phase in which our startup was), the channels of search for money were different; each channel was contemplated in order to find a financing gap that ranged from a certain minimum amount up to a maximum limit. For figures from zero to one million euros, the channel to be used was bootstrapping, i.e. financing through what were called the three effe, namely family, fouls, friends (family, fools and friends). For figures ranging from 10,000 euros up to 2 million, it was seed money: our second channel, the use of which he had actually already illustrated to us and which, our mentor assured, would have supported us in implementing, together with the first channel. Between 2 and 5 million there was talk of growth equity, that is the investment of private capital in the startup, which acquires a minority stake thanks to that loan; this type of financing was specific to expanding companies, for this reason it is also called growth capital in Italy and distinguishes relatively small figures. From 5 to 20 million (figure conventionally established as the maximum financing limit without offer

public) there was mezzanine capital, 2 or loans with subordination constraints in repayment with respect to normal bank debt. These loans are a very complicated tool since in fact they represent a hybrid between pure financing and equity. Beyond those figures, there was no longer talk of fundraising: there were markets (public markets), through which any figure could be reached through a listing on the stock exchange. Apart from this consideration, no one forbids

present sales pitches even for a few tens of thousands of euros to the manager of a fund who is used to financing tens of millions », our mentor emphasized. But the best way remained to use one of these three options:

PUBLIC CALLS - CROWDFUNDING - BOOTSTRAPPING

Of these three possibilities, the first two are feasible through calls and crowdfunding platforms, while the last depends mostly on our entrepreneurial spirit: it is primarily about raising the capital we have and, if that were not enough (or not we want to risk them), ask friends, relatives and anyone crazy enough to give them to us.

Before returning to the story and resuming it starting from the phase in which our mentor tried to convince us that addressing family, madmen and friends, if done following the right formula, did not mean door to door or begging and it was not at all discrediting, I promised my mentor to make this premise, if I ever told this story to anyone, so now you're going to get a SPOILER. 3 Get ready!

In the end we followed all three paths at the same time, because this was the method suggested by our mentor: to take action on all three fronts at the same time and collect what came from the channel that proved most profitable. This is worth repeating, because you must do it too, in your seeding phase:

THE METHOD TO USE

You must activate simultaneously on all three channels:

TO. PUBLIC NOTICES
B.   CROWDFUNDING
C.   BOOTSTRAPPING

... and take funds from all or from the one (or those) that proves to be more profitable!

Taking advantage of every channel, envelope number 3 was the one that earned us the most funding. When I write "the major funding" I mean that the other roads worked too, but in the end the most profitable, believe it or not, was asking friends and relatives for money. Mind you: if they had told me then, I would not have believed it (and I would have probably reacted as you will now!), But later our mentor showed us the right way: organize private presentations to tell our idea through a simplified version. of the sales pitches that are organized for venture capitalists in the other phases of fundraising. Obviously, when he told us about it, we still didn't have the slightest idea of what a sales pitch was and how the various phases of fundraising were carried out, but he assured us that he would explain everything to us in detail. Returning to the story ...

(A few minutes later the missing scene.)

We looked perplexed at our mentor. "I mean ... that is, should I ask my grandmother for the money?"
"It depends: does your grandmother have money to give you?"
"That's not the point!"
"Yes it is. Your grandmother or your best friend are fs, the money to start has to give you the fs you know. "
"Tell me again: who are the fs?"
"However! How easy it is for you to forget what you don't want to remember! " And he wrote again:

FFF
=
Family, Fouls & Friends

"Um ... I would like to point out that we don't know anything about how a sales pitch works, it's the first time we've heard about it."
"You don't have to worry about that: I'll explain everything to you. Let's go back to

the three fs. If you remember well, professional investors finance companies that have produced useful results in interesting times, and a company with zero starting capital has not yet produced useful results; how do you get out? "

We didn't know how to answer.

"The question behind the initial financing is: Who would ever offer money to participate in a startup that has all the excellent conditions to start but does not yet have a spendable execution?"

"Well, if the idea is good, the conditions are there and the request is reasonable ... having the money I would do it!"

«Precisely: only crazy people! And to these madmen like you you will have to turn! The fools we're talking about are actually people who trust you, with whom you have credibility regardless of the performance of that specific company. The formula of the three fs serves to remind us from which circles of acquaintances these contacts of hypothetical financiers come: family members, friends and unconscious lunatics met at the bar! You have to present your idea to this category of people, and convince them to finance you! "

"All right. We now know how to fund the idea from scratch; we know what type of lenders to turn to from time to time and that we must gather everyone in one room to propose the idea to them; however there is still a very small problem to be solved. "

"Which?"

"If I show up from every name in my phone book to ask him for money, I assure you that I won't even get 100 euros !!!"

"Ah, for that matter, I wouldn't give it to you either: first you have to learn how to sell the idea to your financiers."

I started. "And how do you sell the idea to the lenders? What do we have to say to convince them? You yourself explained to us that if we talk about the idea through words we will only receive words of encouragement, while if a man is armed with numbers he will receive numbers. How do we arm ourselves with numbers? What are the right buttons to touch with investors? Is there a pattern for this too? "

«Yes, it's called the sales pitch. If you want to receive money to finance your business project, you need to learn how to pitch a sales pitch. "

"How do you do? Can you explain it to us?"

Our mentor nodded. "Okay, I'll explain how to build an effective sales pitch in order to sell this idea to lenders, but first I have to ask you a question. Depending on the answer you give, I will know whether or not you will get the financing you are looking for. The question is: how is the pedestrian? "

"You are welcome?!" Obviously, I had no idea what he was talking about.

"The pedestrian! I want to know if the pedestrian got away ... "

Lesson n. 7

Fundraising is a constant need. Family, fouls & friends.

FROM THE SHARED FOLDER IN DROPBOX
Crowdfunding platforms
Dear guys, here is a (non-exhaustive) list of crowdfunding platforms: each has its own rules and limitations, go through them and choose one (and not more than one) to use.

Kickstarter: is a crowdfunding website for creative projects; Through Kickstarter, various types of businesses, movies, music, theatrical performances, comics, journalism, video games and food industries have been funded. Unfortunately, it only allows the financing of British or US projects, but the block can easily be circumvented through foreign representatives.

Crowdfunding-Italy: is a generalist crowdfunding platform; registration is free and no commission is imposed on the funds raised.

Produzioni dal Basso: the first crowdfunding platform in Italy, created for

«To offer a space to all those who want to propose their project through the system of bottom-up productions»; it is free and each proposal is managed independently and without any intermediation.

SiamoSoci: it is a marketplace for startups, a "search engine that allows investors to find companies whose business they understand". Through the platform, unlisted companies can raise capital from private investors to finance growth, also facilitating the creation of club deals (group investments) between investors with different professional skills.

We Are Starting: is an equity-based crowdfunding platform.

Prestiamoci: Italian platform for loans between people. It aims to promote the exchange of money between individuals as much as possible, without the intermediation of banks or other credit institutions.

Eppela: allows to finance innovative projects in the artistic, technological and other fields

profit.

Kapipal: born especially for personal projects (including a birthday or a wedding list), it defines itself as "the first international platform to support personal crowdfunding" and does not impose a commission on the projects presented.

Starteed: helps finance your ideas thanks to the Starteed community; in addition to financial support, it also supports the subsequent stages of development and sale, offering the startupper to sell their product on the platform itself.

De Revolutione: is «a platform that allows you to transform your best ideas into

Revolutions, in order to concretely improve the world in which we live»; it hosts both crowdfunding campaigns and petitions and collection of signatures for projects and initiatives of common interest.

Com-Unity: is a generalist crowdfunding platform that hosts projects of any kind but especially in humanitarian, social, cultural and scientific fields. It is made up of an ethics committee, tutors and a bank (founder). The ethics committee evaluates the projects, the tutor assists the planners and the bank manages the sums donated to guarantee donors and proponents.

Kendoo: is a platform to design, create and finance projects according to the all-or-nothing model.

Finance your future: it is aimed at promoting and disseminating new projects for the development of the Apulian territory and was born "from the need to integrate and revitalize the productive sectors of the local economy through the innovation and creativity of young people in the area". Designers can submit a request to raise a fixed amount of 10,000 euros for the realization of projects with a maximum duration of 12 months.

Musicraiser: is a reward-based crowdfunding platform exclusively dedicated to music.

Cineama: is a platform dedicated to cinema.

ShinyNote: it is a platform, but it represents a shared space between non-profit organizations and users created to finance solidarity projects.

Iodono: is a personal fundraising site to allow people to donate online and raise funds for non-profit organizations and causes closest to them.

BuonaCausa: is a crowdfunding platform defined as «the ethic network dedicated to good causes and projects that require support» created to allow associations, companies, donors and activists to collaborate on social initiatives.

Retedeldono: is a platform for the collection of donations in favor of non-profit social projects.

Fund For Culture: is a fundraising system for culture.

Audience Bene: is an experimental investigative journalism project funded by readers and based on the participation of readers and journalists.

Third Value: it is a crowdfunding service through which individuals (resident in Italy) and legal persons (with registered office in Italy) can lend and donate directly to non-profit organizations that are customers of the founding bank.

Smartika: formerly Zopa Italia, offers the possibility of practicing social lending in Italy, in a regulated and supervised manner by the Bank of Italy for the protection of users.

These are just a few, surely you can easily find others ...

Turning to bootstrapping instead, do you remember the environmental enablers of that famous fourth circle? Here, there is a small annoyance to which you must pay attention: the law for offering to the public savings; if you go up on stage, speak on a radio or are a guest on a television program, you cannot say: "If you want a return of X% on your investments, contact me privately". It is not legal.

This is prevented by an Italian law created to protect honest savers from dishonest scammers and direct them to the banks. This law prohibits the public offering of a financial investment: it does not prevent you from proposing a business, however it prevents you from doing it explicitly from a stage to an audience. In practice, during the sales pitch that you will do from the stage, you do not have to talk about numbers and figures, then ask people interested in learning more to provide you with a written declaration of their interest. In summary: you can contact your potential investors individually or organize an official presentation in a hotel; an idea of the costs could be 300-400 euros for the room and around 20 euros per person if you want to go big and organize a reception. This is the form I use for written consent; I am attaching it to you as an example but do not use it without first consulting a lawyer: situations and regulatory contexts vary from case to case. I am inserting this document only in exemplary terms, understood?

METHOD OF PARTICIPATION
Dear
I declare that I wish to participate in the capital increase in favor of third parties as regulated in the specific meeting.

The documents required for the subscription of the fee are:
Individual member:
Identity card and tax code Partner legal person:
Chamber of Commerce registration showing the powers of signature of the administrator Identity card and tax code of the administrator

1 The reference is to those myriad companies born in a garage, of which the best known exponent is Apple, which has made its own brand story.

2 Mezzanine capital is an advanced tool to finance an already structured company that needs money and that has already been financed by banks or venture capitalist funds, and serves to receive even more money: it is basically "debt" capital that gives the creditor has the right to convert into ownership or participation in the company if the loan is not repaid in full within the established time frame.

3 «Anticipation»: it is a typical expression of the web language. This is the notification to users that a certain passage contains a description that could

reveal the ending of a film, a TV series or a book.

Lesson n. 8. Overselling

The threat of misrapresentation
March 16 - 1.00 pm, lunch

Our mentor explained to us that this was a test 1 he had undergone during his stay in California, before meeting the venture capitalists of Silicon Valley; it was a test to understand the cultural barriers between Europeans and Americans. Basically, things worked in the following way.

Scenario

You are a passenger in a car driven by a close friend when he hits a pedestrian. You know your friend drove at 35mph, with a limit of 20mph. There are no witnesses. Your friend's lawyer argues that if you testify under oath that your friend drove at 20mph, he could avoid serious and serious consequences.
Question: What do you think is your friend's point of view?

Your friend has a certain right to expect that you will testify on his behalf. Your friend has some right to expect that you will testify on his behalf. Your friend has no right to expect that you will testify on his behalf.

The test was to answer that one question. The approach, our mentor explained to us, varies according to the country of origin; Americans tend to tell the truth about how things went, as do the Swiss and the Germans; in different percentages, the French and the Spaniards are a little more opportunistic. Among all cultures, there is one that tends more than others to answer the question with another question:

What happened to the pawn?

Since, depending on whether the pedestrian had died, sustained more or less serious injuries or remained unharmed, their response would have changed. It is European culture. And of course, among the Europeans, the people who tended to ask more frequently: "How is the pedestrian?" and to change their approach to the context, it was the Italians!

"It doesn't seem wrong to me", I objected, "on the other hand, if there are no victims ..."

"It is not a question of thinking in terms of right or wrong, only to understand that, since you are Italian, you will be scanned much more than if you came from other countries. Especially in recent years our nation has enjoyed a very bad reputation for honesty and legality. I don't want to go into the matter

politician: I am an entrepreneur and I am explaining to you in entrepreneurial terms what this entails; if the registered office of your company is in Italy, the investment is considered at risk. "

"Well ... isn't Made in Italy a brand that plays in our favor?"

«The made in Italy certainly: however today it is possible to obtain that a product is certified made in Italy even if the company that markets it is based elsewhere. Let's be clear: a team of Italian developers is still well regarded and, in many cases, considered a plus; we Italians, individually, are still considered heirs of the Renaissance and innovative and brilliant inventors, valid workers. It is on the governmental level that we are lacking: compared to those of other states, our governments are not considered stable. "

"But we are startuppers, is the regulatory environment really that important?"
"Do you remember the fourth circle?"
He had outsmarted me: it was true, and we had already discussed it. "Ok, the Italian office may not play in our favor, but for this reason our company is liquid."
"In fact, we have already dealt with the external factor, now we have to resolve the internal aspect: it is a question of cultural barriers."
"Be clearer."
"I will be!" Our mentor stood up, walked over to his office whiteboard and wrote in large letters:

YOU DON'T HAVE TO LY

"To lie? Why should we lie? "
"All startuppers lie during their presentations: you don't have to do that anymore!"
"We don't."
"When you first introduced yourself to me you said you had developed a working beta version, immediately afterwards you corrected yourself by specifying that it was 80%. Now that we work together we know that development is 40%, maybe 50%, but not more: this means lying. "

"Well ... we were nervous."
"Of course, I understand: you were nervous and unprepared. In a few minutes you had to play all the cartridges and you needed to impress, so you bowed the truth a little, nothing more than that: you didn't really lie, just magnified the facts a little. "
"Exact..."
"You must never do that again!"
"But..."
«This is not about a job interview or a delivery: you can't say that you are almost finished when you are still halfway through, or that you only have to solve a small problem when there are three big flaws! You're dealing with venture capitalists! "
The difference escaped me, but I was afraid to ask. He noticed it.
«The difference is that if you lie at an interview, you are lying to your employer: if he falls for it and hires you then it's his own business, not yours; you remain the wrong person who lied, but not the stupid person who did harm to himself. Because the damage you have done to those who are paying you to do a job you don't really know how to do. You are cowardly and

unfair, but it is your choice to be. Likewise, if you lie

because you are late on a delivery so as not to make a bad impression and then you also work at night bringing the work home to catch up, it is a white lie, you do not harm anyone and you are in full power to fix it. On the contrary, when you tell your financing partner that he has a problem, he will move seas and mountains to solve it, exploiting his personal contacts, putting his capital and thinking, legitimized to do so by your lies, that once that problem is solved the business will take off: if it turns out that there were other problems and you didn't list them so as not to look like a jerk, you put both him and you in trouble: lying to a venture capitalist means lying to your partner, and you never lie to your partners ! "
"I get it."
"No, you didn't understand, not completely: what business are you in?"
"Um ... digital entrepreneurship?"
"No, that's just the category to which the product you are developing now belongs: you are in that business."
"Innovative startups?"

"Forget the definitions of the public tender: on which fundamental asset is the sector in which we both work based?"
"I'm sorry: I just can't get there." He wrote in even larger letters:

YOU ARE IN THE CREDIBILITY BUSINESS

"Credibility?" I repeated in a low voice.
«That's right: credibility. We are in the business of credibility! And if you are not credible or you lose credibility, then I am not credible and I lose credibility: so as long as I am carrying you around, you must never lie. It's clear?"
"It is." This time it really was.
"Well, now let's see how startuppers lie."
He explained to us that the reason people lie is the lack of preparation. It was true for the students under examination, for the candidates in the job interview, for the managers struggling with the presentation of their projects: all lie for lack of preparation. Startuppers lie because they are not prepared to support sales pitches. So his job was to prepare us for that kind of interview, but first he wanted to warn us about the main lie we would fall into temptation about: misraprensentation. 2

"Do you know overselling?"

I knew about overpromising, that is, the excess of promises regarding the sale; more or less what happens with teleshopping where you see a knife cut the concrete and stay sharp or a slimming cream that in two weeks of use transforms an obese girl into an underwear model: the ordered product never meets expectations . In that case, we speak of overpromising, as the seller promises the buyer results that the product cannot deliver and creates an expectation that is impossible to meet. I told him.

"Yes, it's more or less similar. In the same way as overpromising, when a startupper tries to 'sell' his company for more than it is, or tries to appear himself

himself better than he is, with more skills and greater insights: in that case we are faced with misrapresentation. Mind you: you can play a little bit in describing the potential of your idea, but when it comes to you and your team, you have to say it as it is! In particular, you must not lie about:

- Time of realization.

- Contracts and agreements signed or negotiated.
- Budget available.
- Your skills or those of your team members.
- Time (yours and team members) that you intend to devote to the project.

We looked at the list, which did not use big words, ambiguous terms or technical jargon that left room for interpretation: it was no good for anyone to lie to venture capitalists, that was the point.

"Is that clear to you?"

"Too much."

The mentor noticed my hesitation. "What's the problem?"

"Many of our development team members work part-time, I would have preferred not to specify that."

"Instead you will specify it: they might see it as an obstacle and decide not to finance you, but they could also offer to provide you with support and you would get an advantage."

"It's hard to find out all the cards right away."

"Choosing to have character is often a hard choice," he smiled. "But if you

choose not to have it, I'll give up right away."
I smiled too, back. He put his hand on my shoulder and his voice became softer and more understanding. For a moment it was a good moment: I felt him almost like an older brother; he looked me softly in the eye and added: "And if I quit you, then they spit you on all the venture capitalists I know." I loved him. I. He loved his investment.

FROM THE SHARED FOLDER IN DROPBOX
Cultural barriers
At the time, I didn't understand the reason for that speech. Now that it has been a long time since that strange question, and that I have given several presentations and dealt with a lot of business in different languages and countries, I understand why that initial test. In general, you should know that there are three reference cultures in business:

- Culture A: Scandinavia - Germany - Switzerland - USA.
- Culture B: Greece - Spain - France - Italy - UK.

- Culture C: Japan - China - Latin America - Middle East.

Depending on the reference culture you use, many things change. For

example in culture C reproach is taboo. I remember an episode in which I found myself berating a Chinese manager in front of his team; it was open feedback and, in the team, I often urged direct confrontation, which in other cultures would have been accepted, but in culture C it is unacceptable: an unforgivable humiliation. And the more I scolded him, the more the victim laughed and laughed and made me angry ... They explained to me only afterwards that laughing when you get a rebuke is, for that culture, the greatest admission of guilt. That poor fellow was literally mortifying himself in front of me and I thought he was making fun of me! Similarly, when I found myself working in a team of Americans, I had a tendency to never complain and to let the limited means available to me suffice; when they pointed this out to me, reproaching me for the fact that I never demanded more resources, I asked for explanations and explained that, while in

Europe "the protruding nail will be hammered", in American culture "the creaking wheel will receive oil". We have to pay attention to cultural barriers when presenting our startups. Now, you might think that these are too simplistic examples: it is due to your reference culture, which is European; consider that the reference culture of startups is instead the American one, therefore a type A culture; and type A culture, simplifies everything. The rules of this world were born and evolved from this cultural cradle, which is why you too will be led, albeit not forced, to align yourself with this basic culture, even if you are European or Asian. For example,

European reasoning = deductive

For Americans, and in general for Type A cultures, the effectiveness of the solution is important: those who linger on the problem are seen as slow or jinxed or ineffective or complication-oriented or not a man of action:

US reasoning = inductive
The sales pitches are mainly developed on the US approach: brief overview of the

problem, pushed sale of the solution we propose and the spotlight focused with enthusiasm on the future, or on the dream we are realizing (ie selling to them). If you feel uncomfortable doing it and feel too much of a salesperson or in-depth, that's understandable. Mediate between what is in your strings, what you deem right and what will be effective. The rest is up to you: the startup is yours!

Lesson n. 8

Do not lie. Never lie. You must never lie! We are in the business of credibility!

1   The test is taken from the book by Fons Trompenaars, Did the Pedestrian Die ?, Capstone Publishing, Oxford 2003.
2   Misrapresentation means "selling yourself" for more than you are.

Lesson n. 9. Elevator pitch

Fifteen seconds to impress
March 17 - 3.00 pm, service lift

In his office, the mentor wrote on the board:

You have fifteen seconds to impress.

Then he asked me to follow him, walked down the corridor towards the elevators, entered and explained to me: "According to a study of proxemics, which is the science that relates the distances of interlocutors to communicative effectiveness, most people he is embarrassed to share the elevator with a stranger, because the distance between the bodies is too close. ' We were actually tight. He was looking me straight in the eye, I looked away and brought it up. «For this reason everyone reads the plate that shows the capacity and weight, to avoid making eye contact with the other passengers; if the descent or ascent is particularly long, then we end up hypothetically calculating the weight of each one. "
"Interesting, but what's the use?"

«You ask yourself this question because you are a startupper, and you are focused solely on your project, bravo! If, on the other hand, you were a serial entrepreneur like me, you would know that there is no useless information, only information that you don't know how to exploit; from this, for example, I created a company called Down-Up: it sells advertising space in lift cabins. " He moved away and let a glimpse of a plexiglass plate with an advertising leaflet inside. "This space," he said, "is rented from the building to Down-Up and resold by the building to the company advertised in the flyer: it earns money for the tenants (who pay for their condominium expenses) and for us."
"Simple and ingenious."
«Don't exaggerate: genius not so much, more intelligent than anything else. Simple, however, not at all: we have been tempted several times to let it go because of the regulations. See all these stickers attacking maintainers? None of them are in order: if we applied the fire regulations, we would have to remove them and fine them, but none does; they would do it to us, however, since we base our core business on this. "

"Regulatory environment again, huh?"
"Yeah, the fourth circle again!"
"Interesting, but why are we in the elevator, where are we going?"
«I wanted to ask you if you are interested in helping me develop the Down-Up project. I need a hand on marketing. "
"Gladly, but I should know more, and then you know ... I don't want to lose focus on my project." The elevator stopped and there was a bell that announced the opening of the doors.
"Oops! We arrived, too bad, I didn't make it in time! " The elevator reached the floor.

"In time to do what?" I asked as I was about to get out of the elevator.
«To entice you without making you think of possible obstacles. Where are you going?!" He stopped me with his arm.
"I'm going out of the elevator, haven't we arrived?"
"We don't have to go out, we have to go back to the floor."
"I do not understand. Where are we going and why are we staying in the elevator? " And why were we going back now, above all ?! But I didn't say that.

"We are not going anywhere: we have arrived; we had to go down and now let's go back to the floor, because 'we have to go back to the floor', that's all. "
I was confused.
"Do you have a business card?"
"Yup."
"Give me that." I handed it to him. She didn't even look at him; he took out his pen, and on the back of the card he wrote:

Down-Up
The advertisement in the lift that pays you back all (or almost) the condominium expenses!
If you are interested call us: 555-123.45.67

Then he handed it back to me.
"Hi, are you interested?" And he invited me to read.
He watched me for the next few seconds as the elevator reached the floor.
He said nothing and neither did I.
Back in the room we sat down and only then did he give us instructions. "First write your idea on a business card; then explain it to me by imagining you met me by chance in the elevator. "
He gave them both a business card.

"Arthur Penn, an amazing director I was lucky enough to meet, once said to me, 'If you can't write your movie idea on the back of a business card, you don't have a movie.' It's more or less the same with business ideas: if you can't summarize them in a small space, you're not clear. "

"Yes, but why the elevator ?!"

"Steve Jobs used this formula: it was called being 'stevezzati', and for many at Apple it became a synonym for layoffs, he met employees in the elevator and, if they couldn't explain their job and what they did during the race. in the elevator, he fired them on the spot! "

"Wow, was he really that cynical?"

«I don't think so: certainly it will not have been a tender one, but I think that this, like anything else, is part of the 'mythology' that Apple have built around the figure of Steve Jobs; it's marketing, but it's a useful metaphor to understand this: the first pitch you need to be able to do is the elevator pitch. "

"Elevator pitch."

"Yes, elevator sales, if you prefer. You have fifteen seconds to impress: what does it do

your startup? "

I turned over the note I had written and showed it to him:

We will forever revolutionize the way you interact with social media!
We are looking for investors: call us!

"Nice!" he exclaimed. "But we don't want to make them smile: we want to sell them a share of the project!"
I nodded and remained silent, convinced it was the best way to ask questions.
"Okay, I'll tell you what's good and what's not with this answer. Let's start with the good things: you have been very concise, good. Now let's move on to the bad ones. "
He took his pen and wrote:

You didn't tell me how. You didn't tell me how long.
You did not specify whether this change will be positive or negative.

"But ... it goes without saying that it will be positive."
"Nothing is discounted, except the offer you will receive if you continue to be so rough: never take anything for granted when money is involved!"
I was silent. He completed the picture:

You didn't give me measurable parameters.

"Are you saying that, in fifteen seconds, we should be able to explain our idea by specifying how, how and by how much, also offering numerical and comparative parameters?"
"Yup."
"Exactly: how many words per minute would we have to say to do this?"
"The least possible. The secret of effective communication is brevity. "
"I understand."
"Make a note of this." The mentor wrote on the board:

The secret of effective communication is brevity ... The secret of effective communication is brevity ... The secret of effective communication is brevity ...
... And repetition!

"Got the concept?"
I smiled. "Yes, you have been effective; now tell me how we do a complete picture in fifteen seconds, though. "

"You don't have to do the whole picture: just entice them to the point of wanting to know more.
Your statement must implicitly shout ":

Do I have your attention, investors?

"And how does a lender get enticed?"
"First I'll explain it to you in theory; later, tonight to be precise, I'll show you in practice: get ready, it will be fun. "
We had no idea what he had in mind, but it sure would have been inconvenient for any of us.
"Basically, you have to think of yourself as a salesman. Most salespeople don't have a sales strategy: they may be good with words and sell thanks to talent and because they knock on many doors, but they don't have a system. Instead, what I want to give you, to sell your idea to lenders, is a sales procedure that works, or rather, that optimizes your chances of successfully concluding that sale. "
Every time he said the word for sale, he made the quotation mark gesture with his fingers. "How come you say 'sale' with quotes?"
«Because it is more than a sale: it is the sale as every seller should understand it;

that is to say that the customer, once closed (or signed the contract) is not to be considered another notch on the shotgun, but a partner with whom to continue the journey, perhaps continuing to sell more. In the case of a seller these are any
upsell 1 but in our case it is more delicate, because we have a partner in the house; this is why it is a more delicate sale, in which lying is at your expense. "

"Yes, you were very clear about overselling."

"That most salespeople don't follow a system is pretty obvious if you know where to look: you can tell by the fact that they can't effectively answer the question: 'What do you do?'"

"In what sense do they not know how to answer?" They will answer that they are salespeople, or commercials or consultants if they are ashamed to be salesmen, but they will certainly know how to give an answer! "

"I didn't say they can't answer, I said they can't do it effectively. I mean that they do not know how to give a short answer, which entices the interlocutor and which clarifies in the meantime what advantage they are able to provide, in what way, how much the improvement will be and

in how long we will be able to obtain it, specifying that the improvement will only be possible thanks to their intervention. "
I wrote myself the various points:

What benefit are they able to provide.
How.
How much improvement will be.
How quickly will we be able to get it.
Specifying that improvement will only be possible thanks to their intervention.

"I have to tell you: if I ask someone what they do, I don't want to be answered with a sales pappardella."
"Of course, nobody wants it. That's why you have to entice you: offer a glimmer of interesting information, you have to give him a snack, not a slice of pizza! "

"You're making me hungry ..."
"It came to you because we talked about a pizza, you imagined it, but I didn't serve you a pizza on a plate."
"No, I got hungry because it's after three."
"Choose, do you want to have lunch now?"
I considered the idea and was about to answer when he added: "Because in the next few minutes I will explain how a

lender gets enticed, in the time of an elevator ride, to the point of convincing him to invest a million euros in your idea, accepting in return a maximum of 40% of the shares ".
"Okay, you convinced me: I'm staying!"
"Did I really persuade you to stay?"
"Yup."
"Do I have your attention?"
"Sure."
"How long did my speech last?"
"What do you mean?"
"I just exposed you to an elevator pitch, I'll tell you again:

In the next few minutes I will explain how a lender gets enticed,
in the time of an elevator ride, to the point of convincing him to invest a million
euros in your idea, accepting a maximum of 40% of the shares in exchange.

"How long did my presentation last?"
"Not even fifteen seconds."
"Yet I mentioned, barely touching it, every point of interest to you, that is to say ..."
He took my notebook for notes and made a check mark on each item on the list, writing next to it the exact words he had spoken:

What advantage are they able to provide → to convince a lender to invest.
How → I will explain it to you.
How much will the improvement be → one million euros in exchange for a maximum of 40% of the shares.
How quickly will we be able to get it → in the next few minutes.
Specifying that improvement will only be possible thanks to their intervention
→ I will explain it, it is you who must stay and hear.

FROM THE SHARED FOLDER IN DROPBOX
Scheme for building an elevator pitch

Every seller must be able to answer this question: "What are you selling?"
But that's not enough. Every self-respecting seller (ie prepared) must also make sure that the response stimulates or invites the interlocutor / potential buyer to purchase (if not directly, at least to know more). It may seem like a detail, but try to have this conversation with any salesperson.
You: "What work do you do?" Him: «I sell».

You: "What are you selling?"
You will almost always get different answers. And in the meantime the elevator arrived at the floor! And, worst of all, most of those answers are not attractive from a sales point of view, that is, they do not entice you, that is, they do not generate the desire to continue the conversation on the part of the customer. Each of your salespeople (i.e. you) must be able to summarize the company's activity in a single sentence that touches the levers of the potential customer and combines them in order to arouse in him the desire to learn more / become a customer of the company. How? Through a very simple wizard that we will now apply. Write down the answer separately.

Question n. 1 - What do all customers want to know about a product? Answer:

If you answered "How much does it cost" you are wrong: that may be the question they ask, but not the information they really want to have. 2 What they are interested in knowing are three factors:
1. QUALITY: Does your product / service improve my situation?

2. QUANTITY: How much will I improve?
3. TIME: How long will it take to get the result?

Point. Only and only this. And you have to summarize the answer to these three questions in a sort of slogan or in a synthetic sentence, which you (i.e. each of our sellers) will have to know by heart, according to this scheme:

1. Who? Our company / us / our product etc.
2. Does what? Positive improvement.
3. How? Through the product / service / our experience / a precise method.
4. How much? Provide a measurable term / numbers / proportions.
5. How long will it take? Specify a measurable term / numbers / aspect ratio. Example

I sell the doubling of the annual turnover and an average profit increase of 20% for companies.

I allow you to open a wellness center by investing less than 10,000 euros and go into profit from the first month.

I help companies to obtain financing between 50,000 and 2 million euros.

I help people get extra income ranging from 500 to 2,000 euros per month by investing four hours a week, working from home.
I propose a zero-risk investment that pays a minimum of 10% per annum with the guarantee of returning the amount invested if the return were to be lower.

Well, now that we have the sales summary and our salespeople are able to explain, it's up to you. Write down the answer separately.
What are you selling?

"Are there any questions?"
"Only one: are you sure it's not overselling?"
"Do you remember when I told you: never lie or exaggerate the truth?"
"I have it carved in my mind."
"Well. The elevator pitch is the only exception allowed to that rule. But sparingly: creating too high expectations is a mistake that you pay for in the next step."

Lesson n. 9

Always have the elevator pitch ready!

1 The term upselling brings together all those marketing strategies aimed at increasing the value of each sale made, not necessarily (or not only) from the point of view of profits, but also of loyalty. Upsell is, to summarize the concept, that sales strategy through which we are able to raise the value of the transaction carried out by orienting the customer to purchase a product or service of greater value than his initial choice. Typical examples of upsell are: the extension of a guarantee, the proposal of a higher category product, the addition of accessories and options on the purchased product. A typical example is the classic question that the McDonald's waiter asks us when ordering: "Do you also want the fries?" or "Do you want the menu?" what does it dogo from buying a simple hamburger to buying a full menu.
2 Steve Jobs often said, "People don't know what they want until you show them."

Lesson n. 10. Sales pitch

Prepare for the three rounds
17 March - 7.00 pm, office

"And what's the next step?"
"The second round!"
"Second round?"
«Just like a boxer, as a startupper you have to be prepared to take three rounds. The first is about the short distance: the time of an elevator ride, and we just saw it. The second is on the medium distance, and is the one in which the idea is presented in the general project. The third is the one in which the numbers are dealt with in practice and the papers are sifted, before signing an agreement. The lenders will want to see if you can handle all three distances. "
"So it's not possible to succeed at the first meeting, at least two more must follow, right?"
"It is not said: there is no rule, everyone does as he pleases with his money; You might meet a millionaire next door at the bar, accidentally talk to him about your project, and find yourself with a check in your hand and a deal signed on a napkin. For example, it has happened to me, but

it's rare... just as it's rare for a boxer to win by knockout in the first round: you train to be prepared to endure all rounds, even if the match could end earlier. "

"Of course, it's clear!"

"What you will almost never know before is what kind of round you are going to face; the question to ask yourself immediately is the following ", he continued, writing on the blackboard:

How long will you have their full attention?

"You mean how long will they receive us?"

"No, I mean how long they will listen to you, not how long you will sit in front of them! The difference is huge: if they don't pay attention to you, it won't do any good to explain your project by talking about it for an hour or more. "

"And it's the same, I guess, if they interrupt us in the middle: if we study a presentation that is too long and we can't complete it because we are interrupted. We will have wasted our chance to get financed! "

"For this reason we use presentations of a standard length and more or less similar

formats: to save time and understand at any moment where we are and what we are doing."
"Of course: if we all speak the same language it is easier to understand each other!"
"Then I'll teach you that language."
"We are ready."

«The first format we said was a presentation lasting from fifteen to thirty seconds, which we called the elevator pitch. You must always have it ready, because you do not know how and when you will be called to use it. For example, I met the Down-Up guys by chance, and I chose to invest in the company right after an elevator pitch; they didn't even know my name or that I was a business angel, but they were prepared to answer my questions and took advantage of the opportunity thanks to their fifteen second presentation model. "
"They caught the ball!"
"Yes, but they could only do it because they had prepared themselves first. Imagine finding yourself locked in the elevator with Flavio Briatore ... "

"I don't like Briatore very much: I wouldn't choose him as a reference entrepreneur."

"Who cares if you don't like him: he's one who gets results!" As a startupper you have a duty to please anyone who is willing to finance you on your terms and does not kill baby seals for a living! "

"Don't get hot, it was like that, just to say ..."

"Imagine who you like, as long as it is someone potentially able to finance you: wouldn't it be better to have something more to say to him than: 'Nice shoes'?"

I smiled. "Kind of like with a beautiful girl."

The mentor glared at me. "It's not 'a bit like', it's 'exactly like'. Backers are seduced and, just like beautiful girls, they are fickle; but, unlike the models, they are not as easy to convince, because in addition to nice words and good looks, they also look at your bank account numbers. "

"Well, sometimes women too ..."

"Yes, but unlike the daughters you hang out with, the financiers know how to read those numbers better; and they will not look at them stealthily trying to deduce the financial capabilities of your business from how you dress, from how you look at the menu or from the car you drive: they will ask you for explanations and you will have to know how to convince them. Trust me, seducing women is easier than seducing investors; beautiful women, at times, may decide to invest in an evening with you even just out of boredom, sympathy or ... pity. A venture capitalist will not do it: he will look at the numbers, the team and how you present it all. "

It was clear. I wanted to know more about how to convince models, but I preferred to focus on the lenders.

«So: what are investors looking for? The answer is: everything. And that all are the following characteristics ... "

He explained everything to us verbally, talking for almost two hours, but I will spare you in the story and summarize through some bullets (as he urged us to do in our presentations to be short and effective, our long-winded mentor).

What do investors want to see in us?

Elements to be perceived during the sales pitch
A strong and clear vision of the project. You have to design a path that considers

the reference market, the socio-economic context, the competition and that leads to monetization: you can do business for passion but passion investors don't care, they want to see that you are oriented towards

profit.
A team with defined roles in which each member has the skills and characteristics required to develop the project. In addition, there must be a leader: a team in which all boys scouts are good at the campsite. Doing business is not a campsite: you have to show that there is a leader who gives direction and makes decisions. During the presentation phase, the leader must demonstrate that he is coachable, that is, listen to the advice of the investors, but also that he has a clear vision of the project: listen to everyone's opinion but then decide on his own and take responsibility.
Execution: that you have been able to bring reasonable results, obtained in an interesting time. A compelling story: because it never hurts.
An honest relationship.

Proper and regular management of financial flows. The feeling that they will not have any unpleasant surprises.
That you have reasonable growth expectations vis-à-vis the market.
Don't think you are successful because you are the best. ("We're the best" is a child's consideration.)

"There are two types of investors you can meet: angel investors and venture capitalists. The difference between the two is that while the former invests his own money, a venture capitalist invests the money of others, that is, he moves capital belonging to companies that he himself controls or manages on behalf of third parties, or funds for which he is a manager. When you meet a venture capitalist, be prepared to go under the X-rays, because whatever money they decide to finance you will be required to justify that choice in front of a board of directors, and will have to answer for it personally, if things go wrong. An angel investor, on the other hand, responds to himself so, as a rule, he is less bureaucrat, but this does not mean that it will be a walk in the park! "

We nodded. "Ok, everything is clear to us: now tell us what tools we need to use."
"Regardless of who you meet, the tools you need to prepare to present your business are the same: the first is the elevator pitch, the rest is necessary ..."
I was tired and I felt discouraged by the idea that the more we would move forward with our startup, the more we would have to go through all that process.
"A miracle?" I said absently.
"No, organization," he replied, tossing my iPad into the air. I caught it on the fly. "Did I wake you from numbness?" Well, now take notes, you need four necessary items plus a couple of optional accessories... "And, for the umpteenth time, he wrote on that hated blackboard.

Essential elements:

Elevator pitch DONE! Business plan. Executive summary. Medium slide deck. Long slide deck.

He wrote DONE after the elevator pitch, because we had already prepared it.
"Beyond that, there are some optional accessories that never hurt."
"And what are they?"

"I should first talk to you about the elements you can never give up on, but since it's a quick topic that's fine, the impressive optional elements are ..."

We took out a pen and paper and got ready to take notes.

"First of all a video (short: two and a half minutes at the most)", continued the mentor,

«Which explains the business idea; very useful especially if you do several presentations or presentations in public. The video must be exciting and smart, easy to understand and with simple language: like an advertisement. It does not necessarily have to contain technical information but it must still explain the numbers behind the business and hint at the market scenario, not just the idea. "

"Very clear: a video that gives a professional image, frames the idea and does not tire the interlocutor."

"Precisely. The second plus is an endorsement, that is to say the presentation by someone who speaks well of you. "

"That is, some kind of hook?"

"If you have it, it's better; this does not mean that without the knowledge you will not go anywhere, it just means that reputation is important and we are more likely to trust someone if they have been introduced to us by a friend who insures for them. "

"What if we don't have anyone to certify our worth?"

"The fact that no one knows you or spends good words for you is in fact already an endorsement, only it's negative: you better find someone!"

It was relevant information: do not snub the search for references.

"Ok, what's the third element?"

"Have a beautiful girl accompany you!" I stopped writing.

"Why would it matter?"

"Because it makes you look cooler. Furthermore, it is more difficult for men of power to be miserly in front of a beautiful daughter: the man of power always has his sex appeal. "

"Well, even the man who shatters another man's dreams demonstrates power: don't we risk destroying us in front of everyone in order to impress?"

"Hey, I didn't say it always works: okay, no pretty girls, but the video and the endorsement make sure you have them, okay?"

I was puzzled, but I still wrote the words video presentation and entry in my notebook.

"Now let's move on to the executive summary!"

"What is an executive summary?"

«If what you want to achieve is a startup, the executive summary is the most important element of your business plan! Even before the numbers, this is what proves that you have done your homework. "

"Yes, but what exactly is it?"

"It is a document that allows investors to see your business idea as you are seeing it: an in-depth analysis of the potential of the idea on the market, summarized by key points ... and at the same time also a path, a story that accompanies them from problem you have identified to the solution you are proposing. "

"So this is a description by key points?"

"Yes, but it is simplistic to understand it this way, since the job of an executive summary is to show your business, not just describe it."

"I understand ..." I didn't understand at all.

"I'll show you." And he wrote on the blackboard:

1. The problem we are going to solve (or the pre-existing need).
2. The solution we propose.
3. The business model of our company.
4. The technology we use.
5. How the market presents itself.
6. Who are our competitors.
7. Information about our company.
8. Information about our team.
9. Financial analysis.
10. Roadmap and timeline.

"The executive summary is a presentation 1 of the startup according to these ten points."
"That's a lot of stuff: how long does it have to be?"
«From one to three pages: you have to be succinct. Remember: the executive summary should serve as a short presentation that clarifies the most important things at a glance. Something deliverable, but that doesn't take more than a couple of minutes to read. And that your interlocutors can bring with them: a memo, so to speak, illustrating the salient

points. Its fundamental value lies in being the text that the potential investor reads first of all, so it must be compelling and capable of attracting attention. If you do not draft it in short form, you run the risk that the investor will not read it at all and immediately move on to the business plan. "

"And why would it be a risk?"

«Because the numbers are cold statistics: you show the numbers without first being persuaded of the goodness of the idea, and nine out of ten investors will think: Why should I embark on this project? Who makes me do it when I can earn a lot more by speculating on foreign funds or in real estate? For this you have to deal with a few, simple key topics: a description of the company (including products and / or services sold), the mission, the management, the target market and the potential customers, the marketing and the sales, the competitors, the steps operational, financial plans and estimates. And on the first or last page, you decide where, insert a catch phrase that acts as an exhortation for investors; some call it a kind of kick in the butt. "

"Like for example: 'Invest in the app of the future'?"

"Something like that, but more aimed at your specific industry."
"I understand that in order to answer the questions in an executive summary, we need to clarify these points to the investor," I said, showing my notes.

What is the problem we are solving. Who has this problem.
Why should he invest in our business.

What plans do we have for the future.
What we seek from him.

«It's a good summary! The first point to address is the problem: describe the problem you have identified. It could be the absence of a service or a way to improve an existing service or the innovative solution to a widespread problem. "

Write down the answer separately.

Executive summary - point 1 - The description of the problem. "Describe the problem you have identified and intend to solve; also explain how widespread it is and who has that problem (our potential buyers). "

Executive summary - point 2 - The solution we propose. «Describe how you intend to solve the problem: what does our company / product do? How? What results and benefits does it bring? "

Executive summary - point 3 - The business model of our company.
«Outline briefly and give a quick description of how you intend to enter the market and plan to monetize once inside. Be brief. "

Executive summary - point 4 - The technology we use. "What tools and means do you use? How replicable are they by others? How fast? Do you have innovative devices or patentable technologies? "

Executive summary - point 5 - How the market presents itself. "Get a quick overview of what the market looks like in general."

Executive summary - point 6 - Who are the competitors. "How fearsome are the competitors? Remember the rule of ten: you must have more than one competitor (if you have only one big one, and it's called Microsoft, change sectors!) And no more than ten! Four to six are ideal. If you don't have competitors, it's not good, it's bad: it means that you are not seeing them or that the business is not there. "

Executive summary - point 7 - How is the company structured? "Where is it based? Who is the shareholder base (explain who the shareholders are and how the shares are divided). "

Executive summary - point 8 - Information on the team. «Make it a team made up of heterogeneous skills (not friends who all have the same background and who have had an idea together) in which everyone compensates. Show that there is leadership: a group of only boy scouts is fine if you have to go camping, not if you have to start a company. Describe the characteristics of each one, going to the point (do not start from the prizes won in middle school to get to the sporting successes: two synthetic lines, please!). Before showing that you are the right team, make sure you really are: it is important to be objective, just like for rock bands, startup teams break up close to the goal and screw everything up! Be

objectives from the beginning: if the crew doesn't work, abandon ship! "

Executive summary - point 9 - Financial analysis. «Insert a short extract of the business plan, which we will see shortly. A summary that highlights the most important numbers: costs and revenues projected over time (years or months), essentially. "

Executive summary - point 10 - Roadmap and timeline. "List the salient steps of your roadmap, which you will develop in more detail in the business plan that we will see shortly."

FROM THE SHARED FOLDER IN DROPBOX
The nine points of an executive summary according to Guy Kawasaki
Dear guys, I have explained to you which points to touch and how, when you write your executive summary; I'm not the only bell though. A bell that rings beautiful notes is one of the few men in the world to deserve the title of Apple Fellow: Guy

Kawasaki, the inventor of the concept of evangelist in consumer electronics. He prefers to break down an executive summary into nine points:

1. The catchphrase: Guy suggests starting with a sentence or two that give the tone of the rest of the document and summarize or introduce why your business is a great idea.
2. The problem: then it should be explained briefly what is the problem that your business will solve.
3. The solution: then you need to show the offer, i.e. what the company does (our product or ours service) and, of course, to whom we turn, therefore to those who offer it. Kawasaki's advice is to use commonly used expressions and terms, avoiding acronyms or other difficult words that may be incomprehensible to the reader. This, the mentor specifies, is the place to explain how the company creates value, within its sector.
4. The opportunity: it is necessary to indicate the target market segment, its size, the expected growth and the various dynamics (i.e. our forecast on the evolutions: how many people or

companies will become customers of the company, what turnover we will reach, how quickly we will grow etc.). Be reasonable and consider that, according to the guru of the summary, the lottery markets in which, if things were to mesh, you "dominate" a niche, are preferable to situations in which you enter a pre-existing market by taking a microscopic part.

5. The competitive advantage: since competition in the market cannot be eliminated, specify what your secret weapon is. Remember that if at the time of presenting the business plana real competitor does not exist, at the time of the start-up they will jump out like mushrooms. Understand and clarify your competitive advantage for yourself and specify it forcefully. Do not try to leverage only on timing: you must have that in mind, but it is not the weapon with which you will convince the investor (not the only one at least!).

6. The model: this is an essential point. Make it clear that the business model is for making money; explain how and why the startup is scalable and

monetizable. Clarify this through 3-5 year financial models.

7. The team: show that you have a team with homogeneous components, well integrated and that complement each other. It is not necessary to show everyone's curriculum, however if there are previous brands to spend, and they are successful case histories, do it.

8. The promise: Remember that the gist of a sales pitch is the promise of high returns. These you must indicate clearly and reiterate them, a secondtime, through key numbers also in anticipation of expected costs and turnover.

9. The request: when you have to request a sum, do it. Be explicit and remember: once you have justified the request through precise numbers, do not play to the low! Better to ask for a higher amount than what you need, than less than what you need.

«Once the executive summary is finished, give it a nice layout, but don't overdo it: it's not a task for the teacher, but the presentation of a business. Search the web for some models and get ideas! "
"Well."

"Now that you've answered all the questions, you need to streamline your executive summary."

"What do you mean agile?"

"I mean you have to turn it into a versatile tool; you will not always have the brochure of your business idea with you: you may find yourself having to illustrate it in front of an audience, and in that case what will you do? Will you print as many copies as there are spectators? "

"Of course not: we would prepare a presentation, perhaps using slides."

"That is precisely what you have to do before it is needed: because you will never know when the need arises! There are two slide presentations you need to prepare:

Medium slide deck. Long slide deck.

«Medium slide deck: your business idea, illustrated in ten slides, which cover the same points as your executive summary.

"Long slide deck: your business idea, illustrated in thirty slides, which retrace the same points as your executive summary, in more depth."

"Isn't there a short slide deck?"

"Of course there is: it's your executive summary."
"Ah, right! What about the slide decks? Can't you give us some models? "
«Better not: I should give you dozens of them, because you can use multiple styles and I don't want to risk giving you a single way of doing things; however, if you want to take a cue, look on the net: the site www.slideshare.net is full of slide decks. Refer to those of startups that were actually built: you can find everything around! "

"Ok, well, I'd say we have clear ideas now!"
"Are you convinced of it?"
"Yes, we just have to create our presentations."
"Actually, the most important data is still missing ..."
"Which?"
"You know how to ask for money, that's true. But do you have any idea how much you need it? "
"What do you mean?"
"Before preparing the executive summary and slide deck, you need to draw up the business plan, of which the other documents are a summary."

"The business plan ... in fact I noticed that many points between executive summary and business plan are common, I was wondering what the difference was ..."
"There difference is that, in business plan, those points they come treated more in depth. "
And he gave us a model to follow to prepare a business plan.
"You can follow it to the letter or detach yourself from it, but make sure you touch all points whatever path you choose."

Business plan
I will report here the mentor's instructions.

Insert the logo, if you have one. You can have one created at low cost by searching among both Italian and foreign sites that offer their creativity. However, consider that choosing a good logo is a precise marketing operation. The logo summarizes the image of the company towards both the market and its employees, and must be consistent with our positioning on the market. If you have one, place it on the cover page and on each page of the document as a letterhead. If not, just write the company name:

Describe the business model in ten words or less: take a cue from your elevator pitch.

Summary
If your business plan is particularly long, set up an index so that your lenders can quickly scroll through it and focus on what interests them most. For example:

Summary

Company data

On the first page, enter a good business plan. It must necessarily report the essential data of the company. Write them like this:

It is important that any official document you work on contains subject matter and specifications. This is both to be understood by those who read it and for when you will find it among the sheets to be archived after some time. Similarly, it is important that the document shows the date on which it was drawn up, to understand how up-to-date the information reported is. Here is the subject, the specifications and the date to be reported in your business plan:

Main quantitative elements

A business plan describes a business idea through three factors: information, emotions and numbers. The quantitative elements are the initial data that you will enter regarding the numbers and refer to the breakdown of the company shares and the shares available for purchase for potential investors. Since everything has to be reported schematically, it is advisable to use a table like this:

Initial share capital €
Total transferable value subject to the capital increase €
Minimum unit nominal value €

(for each share) Number of available shares Value% of the share capital
(for each share) %

These are essential elements, nothing complicated: fill in the table by entering the numbers that concern your company.

Similarly, summarize the shareholding structure, i.e. who are the shareholders of the company and how many shares they own:

Name and surname of shareholder or name if legal person Percentage of shareholding

NB If you are planning a startup it is possible that you do not yet have the exact calculation or the skills to estimate the number of shares available, the share value of each share, the share capital. In this case you will get those numbers when you have drawn up the forecast budget (see at the end of this session); if so, leave the data in this table and the next one blank and then return to compile them on the basis of the forecast budget.

Titles and synopsis

The business plan tells a story and, like any self-respecting story, this too will have a title and a subtitle. The title of the business plan shows the name of the company or the brand of the project; the subtitle is a definition of effect: it summarizes the explanation by moving the reader. Think of them as the title and subtitle of a particularly captivating movie or book, but don't overdo it: remember that it's still business. Keep it simple and you will not run the risk of making mistakes.

Business plan title:
"   »Synopsis:

Synthesis

In a few lines try to summarize the project you have in mind, so that those who read it can have a clear and comprehensive idea. If the reading generates questions and doubts rather than a widespread feeling of clarity about the project, the summary has not been drafted in the correct way.
Main features

Just as the synthesis is not for the use and consumption of the entrepreneur but for potentials

investors, in the same way the main characteristics of the business plan do not refer to the entrepreneur who develops the company, but to the investors who evaluate the investment proposal and must therefore first evaluate the risk / return ratio of the potential investment; that is, assessing how attractive, potentially profitable and risky it could be to invest in the business.

The three essential elements to consider for an initial evaluation (which therefore must never be missing in any of your business plans) are: the evaluation of competitors, the distribution of income and corporate governance.

Competitor evaluation - Competitors are your direct competitors: those who offer the same product / service or an alternative product / service on the market. To understand if the company you identify as a competitor is your real competitor, you need to ask yourself:

1. Could a customer who comes to me decide to turn to him for the same product / service?
2. Could your customers become my customers to meet the same needs?

It is important to clarify this concept because it is not enough that the product concerns the same field to have a competitor. Think for a moment of the car sector: a used car salesman does not have a competitor of his own in the Mercedes dealer; in the same way a high-profile law firm has no competitor in the cheap lawyer, and this applies to every other sector, from specialized clinics to family doctors. We will deepen this concept when we go to work on identifying the reference target. The evaluations you will have to make will concern: what they offer, who they are targeting, how they are organized, how they reacted or do you think they will react to your entry / expansion on the market, what unites you to them, what differentiates you, why customers should choose you rather than them, and if the market offers enough space for both. In summary: are they a potential threat to your business?

NB Make a list. Where are? What differentiates you?

Distribution of proceeds - In this item you will need to clarify how the company will distribute the money collected. Basically, your potential investors want to know how much return to expect for every euro of profit. That's all. The distribution of proceeds will depend in part on the employee compensation strategy, expenses, how you set up cash flows, which is why the summary you need to enter in this session is a simple summary that makes it clear how much of what is collected will be redistributed among the shareholders.

Corporate governance - This term means nothing more than corporate governance. In practice, it is a question of describing how the company is organized at the level of the management structure: who is in charge of what? What roles are there? The ideal is that not only the foreseen figures are reported, but also the names and surnames of those who hold or will fill these positions. If you consider it significant, include it in the business plan

also a reference card of these people: sector of origin, experience, peculiarities, etc.
In the light of what you have read, and using the following scheme, report in writing a summary evaluation of these three characteristics:

Evaluation of the main competitors:
Distribution of income:

Corporate governance:

NB Even if all markets have similar aspects, each market has its own rules that distinguish it: add autonomously according to your personal assessments the elements that you consider important for the purpose of evaluating the business.

Swot analysis

Any self-respecting entrepreneur is aware of their strengths and areas for improvement and their business. In addition to clarifying them, good entrepreneurs know how to explain them, contextualize them, motivate them and, if necessary, make them attractive. The same applies to weaknesses: they must be clarified, analyzed, reduced and, if necessary, minimized.

Fill in the two lists with the strengths and weaknesses of your business:

Opportunities / risks

The risk / reward ratio is the key to evaluating an investment. Both aspects must be listed separately in this section. It goes without saying that the opportunities must have a greater weight than the risks and, possibly, be greater in number. Imagine that you are facing a scale, as in the case of the following diagram:

On the swot analysis, our mentor underlined: "Obviously, every investor knows that in all business plans, and yours is no exception, you will maximize the strengths and minimize the weaknesses, which will in any case be partially resolved by the way in which you will detail the previous ones. The same is true of risks and opportunities. It is a party game: you cannot avoid playing it ».

Operational strategy

The operational strategy is the description of how the company moves and / or will move (especially in the case of startups or deep corporate restructuring) on the market to achieve the expected results. It is usually timed over time and punctuated by months on an annual basis. It is the one that is included in the executive summary, in the form of a roadmap & timeline.

Briefly describe the operational strategy for the next twelve months using a table like this:

Month Strategy Initiative Monthly result Total result

Operational plan

Alternatively or in addition to the operational strategy, you can also enter the operational plan. It differs from strategy in that it is a description by points (possibly consequential or at least chronologically grouped) of "actions to be taken" and conditions to be created in order to confirm the forecasts of turnover.

Financial analysis

When we got to talking about numbers, our mentor gave us a ten minute break; the issue of numbers, he declared, needed our full attention. When he spoke again he said: "The biggest pitfall for a budding startupper is optimism!"

"Should we be pessimistic?"

«It is not enough: you must become apocalyptic! Do you know Arthur Bloch? He is the author of a series of hilarious books known as Murphy's Law. "
"Yes, I read them: hilarious!"
"The main assumption of all the philosophy behind Murphy's Law is: if something can go wrong, it will. Here, you begin to consider Murphy an optimist: because things are going to get much worse for you and in a way you don't even expect! The venture capitalists with whom you made an appointment to sign an agreement will die the day before, the companies that had signed commitments to finance you will go bankrupt in a week and if things go well your own partners will cheat you, or the idea will struggle. starting or the laws will change or you will have a heart attack while in bed with the two Ukrainian models you selected for the web launch campaign. "
"Here, I wouldn't mind the last one."
"The rule is: double your expenses, halve your income, dilute your time." I wrote:

Double the outputs. Halve your income. Dilute the times.

"Most startuppers want to do the proverbial wedding with dried figs, do you know this expression?"

"Yes, it means going to the savings."

"You have to think big when it comes to budget: you will always have time to cut expenses. But you have to know how to do it with awareness: you cannot overestimate the cost of a resource or an item, otherwise you will only get negative results. They will think that you are naïve who, at best, put numbers at random or that you get fooled by the first one who presents you with a quote or, even worse, that you want to raise money thanks to the venture. "

"And how are the exact calculations made instead?"

"Now I'll give you my procedure: it's just a technical thing."

"But why should this concern us? We are creative, not accountants! "

"If you don't make the numbers work for you, they will work against you! What I am about to teach you is not just basic corporate finance: it is the formula for turning your creative ideas into reality through numbers! "

"There's a problem though ... I've never been good at math."

«What I will teach you does not require notions of mathematics: just the basic arithmetic you learn in elementary school. If you are able to understand that 1 + 1 = 2 then you have everything you need to use the tools I am about to give you. When the calculations on a budget become too complicated to read, it means that whoever draws up that budget either doesn't know how to do it, or doesn't want you to understand what's written on it. "

"Why would a person draw up an incomprehensible bill?"

'Have you ever tried to read a phone bill? It is easy to understand how much you have to pay, but not exactly what you are paying: if it were clearer, do you think most people would rent modems and phones from management companies? "

"Ah ... and I was feeling stupid because I couldn't read a bill ..."

"Jokes?! I know how to compare the balance sheets of Apple and Microsoft, but even I can't understand what I pay my manager every month! I gave up and now, when I can, I use the office phone. "

"And how do you ..." I didn't finish the sentence because the mentor started writing on the blackboard and I got ready to take notes; we would have thought about bills and telephone contracts during the break.

«We start from the principle that, to draw up a budget correctly, you don't need to be good at mathematics; however, you need three estimates to explain your idea from an economic-financial point of view."

- Financial estimate: evaluates the fixed assets (plants, equipment, software, etc.) required in the start-up phase and the working capital necessary to support the initial management costs. The entrepreneur must evaluate:

- how much money is needed to start the business (financial needs);
- if the equity capital is sufficient and if it is also necessary to resort to third party capital (banks, financial companies, etc.).

- Sales estimate: to determine the revenues of the future business, you must know how to predict how much you will

sell. Determine the expected level of sales, think about what should happen to achieve those sales, and identify threats that could jeopardize the achievement of that result.
• Economic estimate: this is a prospectus similar to the income statement and serves to determine the convenience of the business project; in fact, the profit of the future business is determined by identifying costs and revenues.

"It sounds pretty boring," I noted.
"It is. But since it is a startup you must also include in your calculations all the expenses related to the establishment of the company and structural investments (furniture

of offices, plants, machinery, etc.), salaries, any deposit for the rent, expenses relating to consumables and an indication of the equity capital. Only in this way will you have a clear picture of the financial scenario relating to the following months and the ability of the project to remunerate the invested capital. Regardless of the taxes you will have to pay and the tax regime, you will have costs that affect the operation of the business, that is, making it stand up. These are what you need to focus on at this stage. The important thing to understand is: a company has many costs, taxes, bureaucracy; you will only notice most of the costs once you leave. However, you need to get a rough idea of how much it will cost to build and make your project stand. The simplest way to do this is through a forecast budget. A forecast budget is a forecast of the costs you have to incur to get started and stand up for the first time, and it also includes the revenues you will make, not just the expenses. Drawing up a budget is not very different from drawing up an income statement, the only difference is that the numbers must be assumed, because you are not really paying those expenses. Obviously the numbers should not be entered at random. Precisely for this reason it is useful to draw up a forecast budget: because it forces you to inform yourself about costs and revenues that you do not know, highlighting your shortcomings. So, regardless of whether or not you will present the idea to financiers, drawing up a forecast budget will be useful for you to build the company. " A forecast budget is a forecast of the costs you have to incur to get started and stay on your feet in the early days, and it also includes the revenues you will make, not just the expenses. Drawing up a budget is not very different from drawing up an income statement, the only difference is that the numbers must be assumed, because you are not really paying those expenses. Obviously the numbers should not be entered at random. Precisely for this reason it is useful to draw up a forecast budget: because it forces you to inform yourself about costs and revenues that you do not know, highlighting your shortcomings. So, regardless of whether or not you will present the idea to financiers, drawing up a forecast budget will be useful for you to build the company. " A forecast budget is a forecast of the costs you have to incur to get started and stand up for the first time, and it also includes the revenues you will make, not just the expenses. Drawing up a budget is not very different from drawing up an income statement, the only difference is that the numbers have to be assumed, because you are not really paying those expenses. Obviously the numbers should not be entered at random. Precisely for this reason it is useful to draw up a forecast budget: because it forces you to inform yourself about costs and revenues that you do not know, highlighting your shortcomings. So, regardless of whether or not you will present the idea to financiers, drawing up a forecast budget will be useful for you to build the company. " and it also includes the revenues you are going to make, not just the expenses. Drawing up a budget is not very different from drawing up an income statement, the only difference is that the numbers have to be assumed, because you are not really paying those expenses. Obviously the numbers should not be entered at random. Precisely for this reason it is useful to draw up a forecast budget: because it forces you to inform yourself about costs and revenues that you do not know, highlighting your shortcomings. So, regardless of whether or not you will present the idea to financiers, drawing up a forecast budget will be useful for you to build the company. " and it also includes the revenues you are going to make, not just the expenses. Drawing up a budget is not very different from drawing up an income statement, the only difference is that the numbers have to be assumed, because you are not really paying those expenses. Obviously the numbers should not be entered at random. Precisely for this reason it is useful to draw up a forecast budget: because it forces you to inform yourself about costs and revenues that you do not know, highlighting your shortcomings. So, regardless of whether or not you will present the idea to financiers, drawing up a forecast budget will be useful for you to build the company. " because you are not really paying those expenses. Obviously the numbers should not be entered at random. Precisely for this reason it is useful to draw up a forecast budget: because it forces you to inform yourself about costs and revenues that you do not know, highlighting your shortcomings. So, regardless of whether or not you will present the idea to financiers, drawing up a forecast budget will be useful for you to build the company. " because you are not really paying those expenses. Obviously the numbers should not be entered at random. Precisely for this reason it is useful to draw up a forecast budget: because it forces you to inform yourself about costs and revenues that you do not know, highlighting your shortcomings. So, regardless of whether or not you will present the idea to financiers, drawing up a forecast budget will be useful for you to build the company. "

"Ok, let's get this tooth out: what should we do?"

"Draw up a budget."

«A forecast budget? That's all? A single document? "

"To get a rough picture, yes. The forecast budget is nothing more than the company's income statement: in other words, it is the calculation of income and expenses. "

"It sounds less complicated than anything you described above."

"It is! You don't have to become an expert in finance and business economics, just be able to understand, calculate and know how to read the numbers that really interest you.

What he had just said reassured me.

"In practice, it is a question of calculating revenues, costs and subtracting costs from revenues to obtain the net profit, that is, what will remain in the company's coffers once it has incurred the expenses and obtained the compensation."

I took notes:

Calculate revenues. Calculate the costs. Subtract the costs to obtain the net profit from the revenues. Net profit = how much will remain in the company's coffers once it has incurred expenses
and obtained the compensation.

"Here's how you have to proceed," the mentor continued. And as always, I'll tell you about it for convenience.

STEP N. 1

Open a spreadsheet (Excel file or similar). Leave the first column blank and start filling in from the second: column B.
Starting from the second column, at the top of the horizontal axis, we will enter the months; you can decide to draw up the budget for the first three months, the first six or the first twelve months of the company's life.
As the last column, enter the totals column, which represents the complete period.

MONTH 1 MONTH 2 MONTH 3 TOTAL QUARTER

STEP N. 2

In the first column we will insert, vertically, the various items of our budget. Each of these items will be divided into categories: the first category that we will insert will be the income.

The income depends on our type of business: they are all those products or services that bring, directly or indirectly, money into the company's coffers.

Among the entry items there may be the products sold, the consultations provided, the services provided, any down / cross and upsell. In short, everything that brings turnover to our company.

MONTH 1 MONTH 2 MONTH 3 TOTAL QUARTER

REVENUES

Item 1

Item 2

... TOTAL REVENUES

Note 1. If your startup does not expect initial revenue, because it will monetize after a very large population or spread, budget until the time of population.

Note 2. If the monetization will take place after years (not the achievement of break even, the first receipts), still draw up a forecast budget for yourself and enter amounts that vary "for years", rather than months. Undo the final column.

STEP N. 3

The second category that we will include in our budget is that of releases.

The expenses are in turn divided into two sub-categories: fixed expenses and variable expenses.

Enter the variables first, then the fixed ones.

MONTH 1 MONTH 2 MONTH 3 TOTAL QUARTER

REVENUES

Item 1

Item 2
... TOTAL REVENUES VARIABLE EXPENSES

Item 1

Item 2

...

TOTAL VARIABLE EXPENSES FIXED EXPENSES

Item 1

Item 2

...

TOTAL FIXED EXPENSES

STEP 4

Now we will enter the total expenses and the total profit.

The first indicator is obtained, as is obvious, by adding to the total of the variable expenses the total of the fixed expenses.

The second indicator, also quite obvious, is obtained by subtracting the total expenditure from the total income; the resulting figure will be the net profit.

	MONTH 1	MONTH 2	MONTH 3	TOTAL QUARTER
REVENUES				
Item 1				
Item 2				
...				
TOTAL REVENUES				
VARIABLE EXPENSES				
Item 1				
Item 2				
...				
TOTAL VARIABLE EXPENSES				
FIXED EXPENSES				
Item 1				
Item 2				
...				
TOTAL FIXED EXPENSES				
TOTAL EXPENSES (Fixed expenses + Variable expenses)				
TOTAL PROFIT Total revenues-Total expenses)				

STEP N. 5

As a last step, we will put the numbers within our budget.

Since this is a forecast budget, what we will need to do is a forecast for each item in our budget of what we think will occur during the year.

Usually, the question that entrepreneurs ask themselves is: "How do I know how much we will spend and how much we will collect?"

Followed by the question: "Assuming I can predict numbers, how can I know if those numbers are right?"

The answer is that those numbers must be able to predict them based on the study of the market that you have carried out, and more precisely based on one or more of these four factors:

1. The market trend in general.
2. Competitors that you have identified as your particular competitor.
3. The results you have already achieved in that field (if you have already achieved them).

4. Your ambition.

The latter is not the only one you need to consider, it is only part of the equation.

The part about the numbers went smoother than expected: it was the aspect I feared most, but it turned out to be extremely simple and easy to understand. Our mentor was also satisfied: «Once you have calculated the numbers, put them in your presentation along with the rest. To make everything less cold, you can attach the executive summary to the business plan as the first page ».
"And the slide deck? When will we use it?"

"The ten-slide average presentation is usually used for the second match, while the thirty-slide presentation will be used when you have about forty minutes to illustrate the project: generally you get to this phase in the third and last match, following which the foundations are laid for an agreement in principle. In addition, the thirty slide presentation will be the one you will use to illustrate the project during the bootstrapping sales match, with your family, fouls & friends; instead, the short and medium presentation can also be used during startup weekends or other similar events. "

"Startup weekends?"
The mentor smiled: "Eh, eh, eh ... I understand, let's talk about networking ..."

FROM THE SHARED FOLDER IN DROPBOX
What is the decision-making process through which a venture capitalist decides to finance our startup?
Dear guys, here are ALL the steps a fund takes before deciding whether to finance you or not:

1. Endorsement: a presentation from someone who knows you is usually the best way to reach a lender; you have to get used to establishing this type of relationship.
2. Screening session: carried out on the documents provided by the startup and on research carried out by the lender; the startuppers are not present and are not consulted at this stage.
3. Meeting with the partners: after the first, almost informal meeting, a second one follows with the rest of the team that directs the startup. Remember that ventures never look kindly on those

who work alone: the startup is not made by just one person!

4. Due diligence process: the English expression due diligence identifies the investigative process that is put in place to analyze the value and conditions of a company or a branch of it, for which there are intentions of acquisition or investment. It consists in the analysis of all informationrelating to the company subject to the acquisition, with particular reference to the corporate and organizational structure, al

business and market, critical success factors, commercial strategies, management and administrative procedures, economic-financial data, tax and legal aspects, potential risks. She is very painstaking and hard to sustain.

5. Drafting of the agreement: this is the drafting of the contractual terms. This is when an agreement is signed.

6. Disbursement of the loan: it is the beginning, not the end of the relationship; from this moment on, the startup is no longer ours but jointly owned with the lender.

Could you skip any steps? As I have already explained to you, obviously yes: it may happen that you find yourself in your hand a check after a chat at the bar, but the more serious things get (i.e. the more money you ask for) the more this probability becomes remote.

1 You can use PowerPoint, Word, or whatever program you prefer; search the web for some examples to get an idea of the style to use or download the models we have prepared for you from the website www.lorenzoait.com

Lesson n. 11. Networking

Seduction techniques
March 17 - 10.15 pm, in an American bar

I was on my second mojito. Our mentor had given us an appointment in a place frequented mostly by models, rampant professionals and young people. The kind of environment you expect to spend the evening in if you want to find a boyfriend; sure you should be a nice girl first and we weren't. Later we moved to dinner in a place that somehow belonged to a chain of restaurants for which he had overseen the commercial expansion and finally we moved to this American bar particularly crowded with beautiful daughters. I didn't mind it but I didn't understand the connection with our startup projects. We had to talk loudly because of the music, so I shouted my question directly to him: "You said you'd introduce us to networking ..."
"That's what I intend to do!"
"But we are among twenty-year-old boys ..."
"Correct you: we are mostly among twenty-year-old girls."

"Don't get me wrong, it's not that I don't appreciate it, but how can these people help us finance our startup?"

"You can never know if you are facing a millionaire or a middle-class one: you cannot judge by appearances; there is a study called 'the millionaire next door' which tells of how 90% of the rich are apparently normal people at first glance. Do you see that? " and pointed to a very pretty blonde leaning against the bar counter.

"Yes, who is it?"

"I have no idea, let's go and find out!" and before I could do anything she grabbed me by the arm and dragged me to her. The girl turned and gave us the coldest gaze that had ever landed on me.

"Hi, my friend wanted to ask you something ..." then he was silent and stared at me. It was embarrassing. I was standing in front of her and probably exuding embarrassment. The blonde saved me from silence by speaking to me.

"What did you want to ask me?"

I couldn't think of anything relevant and took refuge in the first cliché that came to my mind: "Come ... do you come here often?"

It took him a nanosecond to dismiss me with a: "But please ..." and moved a few meters ahead, to the opposite corner of the counter; I hadn't even plagued his row of stools. I went back to our table dejected, the mentor had just ordered another round of drinks.
«I am offering this: it is to be forgiven! What did you say to make her escape like this? "
"Nothing, a cliché ..."
"Ouch! Don't you know that clichés never work? What did you jump into

head?"
"Well, I was embarrassed, in a cold mind I would never have done it but ..." I realized that I didn't have to justify myself at all. "How did it occur to you rather to frame me like this?"
"Didn't you like it?"
"Jokes? Should I die tonight cream my body and sprinkle the ashes on her! But weren't we here to learn the basics of networking? "
"These are the basics of networking: you just learned the fundamental rule!"
"What would it be?"

"That tension plays tricks on you: didn't you say you know that clichés aren't used to pick up girls?"
"Yes, I said it and I can confirm it!"
"Then why did you use one?"
"Because I didn't know what else to use ... I couldn't think of anything funny to say."
"Now does it occur to you?"
"Yes, but the girl is gone now!"
"Leave her alone: you didn't even know her and here she is full of beautiful girls, stay focused on what I'm about to tell you: the stress brings you back to the level you are used to being."
"Huh?"
"Stress makes you get back into habits!"
"Thing you said?"   Not   the   I
understood   to   cause of the music
         that   It was   raised suddenly.
He wrote on a napkin:

IN MOMENTS OF STRESS DO NOT DO WHAT YOU KNOW YOU SHOULD DO, DO WHAT YOU ARE USED TO DO!

The music faded away and we came back to hear each other without having to shout.
"It's an interesting concept ..."

«This is the reason why athletes train until they become 'stupid': they have to start reacting instinctively, without thinking, to make a technical gesture that is anything but spontaneous, even under stress, become natural. You can also see it like that. " He picked up the napkin and crossed out the word accustomed, replacing it with another:

IN MOMENTS OF STRESS DO NOT DO WHAT YOU KNOW YOU SHOULD DO, DO WHAT YOU ARE USED TRAINED TO DO!

"Okay, but what does this have to do with networking?"
«It has to do with startups, fundraising and everything we've done lately: from elevator pitches to sales rounds. If you get stressed out, you go back to being the hopeless fool who proposed me an NDA at the first meeting! "

"Ok I understand. And what do we actually have to do now? "
"In practice, this is your elevator pitch for tonight," he said, writing one

sentence on the other side of the napkin and handing it to me:

SORRY GIRLS, CAN I ASK YOU A QUESTION?
I NEED A FEMALE OPINION ...

"And what should I do about it?"
"Memorize it, then go to a group of girls (there must be at least two) and use it as an opening sentence. It will work, trust me!"
I discovered that our mentor was also, for hobbies and personal inclinations so to speak, a profound connoisseur of pickup art techniques, which applied advanced principles of marketing and sales to seduction. That apparently harmless sentence actually worked in the same way as an elevator pitch: enticing, but without leaving room for many objections, while communicating about me, in a few seconds, to the investors that:

- I wasn't like the other males in the club (my opening line was unusual).
- I was interested in women's opinions (another unusual thing).
- I was interested in their opinion, not their appearance.

- I had a topic they could talk about, but unless they opened up to me they would never know which one.

Definitely a great elevator pitch! The first girls I approached said yes, and at that point it was panic, because, once again, I didn't know what to tell them; but it didn't go as bad as the first time. I returned to the table less disconsolate and more aware.
"How did it go?"
"Better. Explain to me what the hell should I ask two strangers for an opinion? What do I invent to not look like an idiot?"
The mentor smiled, picked up the napkin and began to draw the sales pitch for the second round.
"Ok, they came to see your cards, now you have to prove that you are not just talk, your slide deck works like this ..."
I could overlook the scheme used by my mentor, but I would not like to receive dozens of emails from the male audience, so I will report below the procedure we used that evening.

Icebreaker question (to be given to at least one couple): «Excuse me girls, can I ask you a question? I need a female opinion».

to) If they answer "yes" ask the following question: "Would you date a girl who still sees her ex, but only as a friend?"

b) If the one to whom you asked the question answers "no", she looks at the other and says: "I understand, she is the cold one of the group (smile); I can count on you?" And ask the question in point a) without giving it time to answer.

Whatever the answer, look at the girl you DON'T like and ask, "May I ask you why?" Listen to the answer, then ask, "You've been friends for a long time, haven't you? Because I noticed that ... "

to) If they have looked at each other before replying, continue the sentence like this: "You look at each other before answering", which is a typical thing that friends do when they have a lot of confidence in each other ...

b) If they have not looked at each other before answering, continue the sentence with: "Don't look at each other before answering", which is a typical

thing that friends do when they have a lot of confidence in each other ...
Walk away saying: "Now I have to go to my friends but I would like to continue talking to you, don't run away, okay?" (Leave them alone so they have time to talk about you and share their impressions, without giving the impression that they need to stay at all costs; come back after a while, acting like an old friend.)

We had a nice evening; leaving the room, I folded the napkin and kept it.
Even now it is framed and hung on a wall in my office. 1
The day after

My head still hurt. My mentor, on the other hand, seemed sprightly and perky even though it was early morning.
"How did it go?" I raised my thumb positively.
"Well, let's try to make today's meeting go well too!"
"Where do we go?" I asked.
"At a startup weekend."

I looked at him with my usual interlocutory gaze that by now he knew very well, in fact he didn't even wait for me to ask him the question to answer me: "It's a workshop that lasts a whole weekend to which startuppers sign up with their projects: they are organized by incubators and, usually, the winners receive aid in the form of funding or other ".

"It looks fantastic!"

"Less than you think. Most of the time you just waste a lot of time, but you meet interesting people, especially if you know who is organizing it and who you have to meet: we go there to meet a particular person, not to participate. "

"Who?"

He showed me the cell phone with the web page loaded on a guy's profile; there was also the photo.

«He could be the right person for your startup; do you remember your elevator pitch? "

"The one about female opinion?" I asked smiling.

"Fool, the one for your company!"

"Obvious that."

"And do you have the slides with the medium and long presentations loaded on your iPad, if they need to be used?"
"Of course."
"Good, let's go!!"
The guy we went for didn't show up at the seminar. However, we encountered other interesting subjects that we did not think we would find. My mentor knew them and told them about me; I hinted at my elevator pitch almost casually, with it

nonchalance trained the night before, session after session, in the room between a set 2 of girls and another; they were immediately enticed by it and gave me an appointment within two weeks.
"Do you see how easy it is?" the mentor told me on the return trip. In fact it had been.
More than meeting girls in a club, even if less fun.
«What you have to do now is to work in an organized way, moving on three fronts. First of all you need finances to get started, so bootstrapping is the watchword; compile a list of people who could become the family, fouls & friends suitable to finance you and make them listen to your elevator pitch: by now you

should have learned to create the opportunity to meet and feel the right moment to do it. Then, with those who are interested, organize a plenary or individual meeting to show them the long slide deck. Finally, to those who declare themselves explicitly interested, illustrate the business plan and propose financing. "

"It's all very clear, I'll do it!"

"Well! I remind you that this is not the way in which startuppers finance themselves: it is the way in which I teach them to do so, so if you think of other ways or you come to know more effective ones, you are free to follow them. "

"Agree. But I will mostly follow your method for now. "

"And since my method presupposes working on seeding at the same time, it looks through the calls to participate in and identifies the events in which to meet crowdfunding platform managers and angel investors."

"How do I find out who the people to know are and where and when the events take place?"

"This is part of the game; it is the networking job that a startupper must learn to do: read magazines, browse websites, search social networks and forums to find out who leads which fund and who moves which threads. Stay informed: get in the loop. I can help you with my knowledge, but don't rely on it alone: you don't have to become dependent on me. "

"I won't be!"

"Remember: there are only six degrees of separation between us and anyone in the world; there are only six people between you and the president of an investment fund. The difficult thing is not talking to them, but convincing them to listen to you! "

"I'll make it!" We said goodbye and agreed not to see each other for a while. I should have used the teachings I received on my own. I had to do that training of mine, after which we would meet again and I would update him on the progress. As I walked away and felt the engine of his Porche Convertible go away, I realized that I had completed my training. I had all the tools, I knew how to move and, although I had just learned about the rules of that very complicated world that were startups, I felt that it was my world and that I had all the tools available to explore and live it. Now it depended only on me. I was finally ready to fail! 3

1   If you were to hang out in my office: it is the picture that has the brass plate that says ELEVATOR BITCH; it's a silly play on words that I'm not going to explain to you ...
2   In the context of the social sciences, a set is the group of people involved in a relational setting. In social and real dynamics, opening a set means interacting with other people at theaim to develop a dynamic of interaction.
3   If it sounds bad to you, it's only because you still think like the rest of the world, rather than as a startupper!

Lesson n. 12. Exit

Intelligence work
March 21, 11.00 am

At the end of the third week we were destroyed; I had held over ten elevator pitches and informal presentations. We had even met with the venture capitalist whom we had not been able to cross the previous time with the mentor in what he himself would have called "a swim in the shark pool". I wanted to lock myself in a dark room and never leave it again, my head hurt, I was full of doubts about my idea that I didn't even find so original anymore and, what is worse, I was full of doubts about myself: felt more as good as in the beginning; we had met teams that were much more dynamic, solid and brilliant than us. It was like going from country fairs to rock festivals,

He smiled. "So, tell me how it went: what did you learn?"

"Our startup is nothing special," I cut short.

"Really? And what else? "

I was silent for a while; I thought back to the dynamics in which I had just participated, to what we had done; how situations had evolved from time to time. No encounter had been at the same level as the previous one, even if all were more or less similar; I had grown up. Getting ready. To observe. Convenient. To listen. To expose. Ask. Define the next step. By now those seven points were done automatically, they had become a way of thinking, a routine.

"I have structured my own system to meet the financiers and exhibit my project."
"Your system? Interesting, teach me. "
"So: there are seven steps", and I listed them:

1. Getting ready.
2. To observe.
3. Convenient.
4. To listen.
5. Exhibit (one of three presentations).
6. Ask.
7. Define the next step.

That seventh point was then reiterated and underlined before leaving, leaving no doubt that it was a question of making a specific commitment, preferably done.

followed by an appointment date and time. The mentor smiled smugly.
"Okay, it makes sense, I like it. I'll steal it from you and teach it to other startuppers, if I get someone willing to learn. But then it didn't go so badly as you say, am I wrong? "
Well, we're not that bad indeed; I found myself thinking that, because I felt like a

nothing; but the state of mind was one thing, my rational mind told me something else: When we expose our ideas they listen to us, and not out of education; we ask questions that arouse their interest, we expose without ...

"I know you finally met him," he said, showing me the photo of the man he told me about the day we said goodbye, the one we tried to cross at the startup weekend.

"How do you know?"

"Why did he contact me: did you mention my name when you spoke to him?"

«Not really, I was with my partner and he asked us which of the two knew you: that question surprised me too. I replied that I had met you some time ago at a presentation pitch, but nothing more than that."

"Um... I must have probably mentioned something to him about you when you were still 'in training'. Congratulations on coming to him without my help - he's not an easy guy to get close to! But it's a shame not to have known it before: you could have played the card of my knowledge: next time, let me know, I could spend a good word!

"I didn't want to cheat, we had decided to speak only in emergencies."
The mentor smiled and agreed with me. We finished the coffee. As we were about to leave, he added: "And tell me, when did you meet him?"
«The first time, 'by chance' at a vernissage that I presided over; I knew he was passionate about modern sculpture and I knew the girl of the artist with whom his secretary had arranged a meeting; the elevator pitch was about two weeks ago, the first round was the day before yesterday. "
"You feel you feel that relationship work you have been able to put into action in such a short time."
«More than anything else it was luck: I tried to approach others too, but it went badly.
Even if I always keep my radars pointed at them ... "
"By the way, GC called me back yesterday. He says your presentation convinced him, I think he will finance your idea. "
It was typical of him: spinning twenty minutes to introduce unimportant concepts and then get straight to the point on fundamental issues.

"Thing?! Are you serious? And how much are you going to put on the plate? "
"How much did you ask him?"
"250k."
"More or less that figure there; maybe even a little more if you play it right. Just wait a good word from me. "
"Then it's done!"
"Are you sure?" A shiver ran down my spine.
"What do you mean? Did you say something that made them think? "
"No not at all. They want to get in, it's just not done yet. For now there is an oral agreement. The steps are these:

- Reach agreement.
- Sign the agreement.
- Keep faith with the agreement.

"And you will realize that it takes a lot of effort to go from one to the other, but for the moment I congratulate you!"
We toasted and said goodbye.

How will it end?
Eventually the agreement was signed. They financed our startup for 245k in exchange for 47.5% of the shares. We kept control by giving, as was the

agreement, 10% to our mentor for the help he had given us; with the proviso, however, that if we needed him we could knock on his door at any time.

For a brief moment, I thought it was really done, but it didn't last long. Almost immediately I realized that having a millionaire as a partner sometimes meant nursing that millionaire: deadlines in payments, late appointments, since we represented just 0.1% of his potential businesses. We were always the expendable commitment. But it was a more than acceptable price to pay to play the game with our project. The biggest problem we had instead a few months later, and that time we risked seeing the project completely wrecked. A very structured multinational had launched a platform that did exactly what we did; when we saw the beta version, it hit me. We spent the next two days staring at my office whiteboard, until I decided to call the only person who could help me. I from my cell phone, he from his, together with the one who had been my mentor and who had now become our partner, we worked in brainstorming all night, to find a way out; towards dawn we were struck by a shock: we found a brilliant way to

transform our being small into an advantage, and the "multinational" structure of our competitor into a burden that made it impossible for it to compete with us. The key was to insert a "social network" dynamic into what was initially born as a static platform. to find a way out; towards dawn we were struck by a shock: we found a brilliant way to transform our being small into an advantage, and the "multinational" structure of our competitor into a burden that made it impossible for it to compete with us. The key was to insert a "social network" dynamic into what was initially born as a static platform. to find a way out; towards dawn we were struck by a shock: we found a brilliant way to transform our being small into an advantage, and the "multinational" structure of our competitor into a burden that made it impossible for it to compete with us. The key was to insert a "social network" dynamic into what was initially born as a static platform.
The result?
The startup I had been running since my first meeting with my mentor?
The million dollar idea I learned was just a tiny part of the cog? It is a social e-

learning platform that, thanks to the problems we have had to face, is now unique in its kind: it allows anyone who wants to teach or learn something to transform that desire into a business. Obviously, for how the startup world works, it will remain unique for a short time: but I hope that, in the meantime, you will hear a lot about it.

Several times, during our meetings, I asked my mentor to collect all his lessons and teachings in a course for aspiring startuppers. Since he never found the time to do it, I did it for him. You can find the material at this address:

Acknowledgments

IF I can live the life I want and be a serial entrepreneur I owe it to the people who work with me and thanks to whom I can carry on my companies without being physically present: I can count on people in whom I place all my esteem and trust, and I also wish you to meet such special people. Thanks to Silvia Marrazzo, my personal assistant, as well as an extraordinary business coach and entrepreneur; thanks to Gianluigi and Francesco Ballarani, precious friends and partners, who embody the philosophy of a modern and liquid entrepreneur more than anyone I know. Thanks to Gianluca Massini Rosati and Alfio Bardolla: they create «Automatic Companies»... since they make me do everything! Thanks to Leonardo Solla, without whom our aesthetic franchise would not exist, I know few people who lend a Ferrari lightheartedly, my friend! Thanks to Massimo Lepore, who with his team of «packman» (Pakistani software developers) solves my problems with 24/7 programming. Thanks to Polyna Kharchenko, it's not easy to get taken seriously in a business world when you're a five-foot model, but you do it very well, it's a pleasure to be your partner! Thanks to Giulio Cesarelli and Giampaolo Faiola, who invented an App to transform car license plates into a chat ... they say it is to help motorists but we know very well that they do it for It's not easy to get taken seriously in a business world when you're a five-foot model, but you do it very well, it's a pleasure to be your partner! Thanks to Giulio Cesarelli and Giampaolo Faiola, who invented an App to transform car license plates into a chat ... they say it is to help motorists but we know very well that they do it for It's not easy to get taken seriously in a business world when you're a five-foot model, but you do it very well, it's a pleasure to be your partner! Thanks to Giulio Cesarelli and Giampaolo Faiola, who invented an App to transform car license plates into a chat ... they say it is to help motorists but we know very well that they do it for "Broccolare" the beautiful daughters at the wheel! Thanks to Alessandro Scotto, who had invented Facebook before Zuckerberg, it's a pity that at the time this book was not there yet... it is with him that we carry on Down-Up. Thanks to Danilo Beltrante, Davide Bonanni, Eduardo Giordanelli and to all the staff of Locobel: it will be thanks to them that the GDP will rise by 1%, they will make Italy "Vivere di Turismo", you will see! Thanks to Giovanni Ciallella, one of the few who can really say that he made the history of Italian startups: your exits are a legend, my friend! Thanks to my father Max, my mother Angela, my first partners, and all the staff of Am.i.co. Srl. Thanks to Francesca Cupane, partner with me in this enterprise called «marriage», and to our little «asset» Alice. Thanks, I love you. Thank you.

www.ingramcontent.com/pod-product-compliance
Lightning Source LLC
Chambersburg PA
CBHW052343220526
45465CB00003BA/929